The Survey of Use of Emerging Technologies in Information Literacy Instruction

ISBN: 978-1-57440-302-2
Library of Congress Control Number: 2014948667
© 2014 Primary Research Group, Inc.

The Survey of Use of Emerging Technologies in Information Literacy Instruction

TABLE OF CONTENTS

25

THE QUESTIONNAIRE

CHAPTER 1 – INFORMATION LITERACY INSTRUCTION TECHNOLOGIES

1. Approximately how many employees at your library provide information literacy instruction or create IL instructional materials?

    A.   1 employee
    B.   2-5 employees
    C.   6-10 employees
    D.   More than 10 employees

2. Approximately how long have you been providing and/or creating information literacy instruction?

    A.   Less than 3 years
    B.   3-5 years
    C.   6-10 years
    D.   More than 10 years

3. Do you provide _____ IL instruction?

    A.   Face-to-face
    B.   Online
    C.   Hybrid (face-to-face and online)

4. Have you created any simple animations (such as GIFs or cartoons) for your IL instruction?

    A.   Yes
    B.   No, but I'm interested and hope to soon
    C.   No, I'm not interested
    D.   No, I'm not familiar with this

5. Do you have a favorite software for developing IL animations?

    A.   Yes
    B.   No
    C.   I'm not making IL animations

6. If you do have a favorite software for IL animations, what is it?

7. Are you using or introducing _____ in your IL instruction?

    A.   Image searching

    B.   Map searching
    C.   QR codes
    D.   Video searching
    E.   Video command searching

8. Are there any mobile apps that you like for information literacy?

CHAPTER 2 – BLENDED LEARNING AND "FLIPPED" CLASSROOMS

9. Have you ever used blended learning techniques in your IL instruction?

    A.   Yes
    B.   No, but I'm interested and hope to soon
    C.   No, I'm not interested
    D.   No, I'm not familiar with this

10. If you have used blended learning techniques in your IL instruction, did you determine your experience to be successful thanks to _____?*

    A.   A formal assessment
    B.   An informal assessment
    C.   Positive student feedback
    D.   It seeming like it went well

11. If you used another method not listed above to determine the success of your blended learning IL instruction experience, please specify.

12. If you have used blended learning techniques in your IL instruction, were they used in _____ instruction?*

    A.   Face-to-face
    B.   Online
    C.   Hybrid (face-to-face and online)

13. Briefly describe a successful blended learning IL instruction experience you have had.

14. If you have used blended learning techniques in your IL instruction, did you use _____ created by you (or the library) in your instruction?*

    A.   Videos
    B.   Readings

---

* Respondents to this question include only those participants who have used blended learning techniques in IL instruction, as per Question 9

    C.   Discussion questions
    D.   Pre-tests
    E.   Surveys
    F.   Online tutorials

15. If you have used blended learning techniques in your IL instruction, did you use _____ created by someone else (other than you or the library) in your instruction?*

    A.   Videos
    B.   Readings
    C.   Discussion questions
    D.   Pre-tests
    E.   Surveys
    F.   Online tutorials

16. If you have used blended learning techniques in your IL instruction and have used in your instruction any other assignments or supplemental materials not listed above, please specify.

17. If you have used blended learning techniques in your IL instruction, approximately how long did it take to prepare this instruction session?*

    A.   Less than 1 day
    B.   1-7 days
    C.   More than 1 week
    D.   Don't know

18. What advice would you give to other librarians interested in using blended learning techniques?

CHAPTER 3 – CLASSROOM RESPONSE SYSTEMS

19. Does your library currently use classroom response systems (popularly known as "clickers") in any of your information literacy classes?

20. If so, which brands do you use?

21. What are your library's plans for classroom response systems?

    A.   Do not currently use nor do we plan to
    B.   Do not currently use but plan to introduce

---

* Respondents to this question include only those participants who have used blended learning techniques in IL instruction, as per Question 9

      C.   Currently use but plan to use it less

      D.   Currently use and have no plans to change usage level

      E.   Currently use and plan to use it more

22. Discuss your library's experience (or your personal experience) with classroom response systems in information literacy instruction applications.

CHAPTER 4 – WRITING CODE FOR INFORMATION LITERACY

23. If your library has developed any unique or particularly effective computer codes or routines for information literacy instruction applications, please describe them.

CHAPTER 5 – GAMES AND GAMIFICATION

24. Have you ever used games or gamification concepts (e.g. digital badges, puzzles, or role playing) in your IL instruction?

      A.   Yes

      B.   No, but I'm interested and hope to soon

      C.   No, I'm not interested

      D.   No, I'm not familiar with this

25. If you have used games or gamification concepts in your IL instruction, were they face-to-face games developed by _____?*

      A.   Your library or institution

      B.   Another library

      C.   Non-library organizations

26. If you have used games or gamification concepts in your IL instruction, were they online games developed by _____?*

      A.   Your library or institution

      B.   Another library

      C.   Non-library organizations

27. If you have used games or gamification concepts in your IL instruction, did you determine your experience to be successful thanks to _____?*

      A.   A formal assessment

      B.   An informal assessment

      C.   Positive student feedback

---

* Respondents to this question include only those participants who have used games or gamification concepts in IL instruction, as per Question 24

      D.   It seeming like it went well

28. Did developing this game require any advanced skills or software (such as programming, graphics, Mozilla Open Badges, etc.)?*

29. If yes, please specify.

30. If you have used games or gamification concepts in your IL instruction, approximately how long did it take to develop this game-based project?*

      A.   Less than 1 day
      B.   1-7 days
      C.   More than 1 week
      D.   Don't know

31. Briefly describe a successful game or gaming activity you have used for IL instruction.

32. What advice would you give to other librarians interested in using games for IL instruction?

CHAPTER 6 – MOBILE TECHNOLOGY

33. How has your college used tablet computers, smartphones, and other mobile computing technologies in your information literacy efforts?

34. Would you say that the rise of tablet computing, smartphones, and other mobile computing technologies has significantly impacted your college's purchasing plans for hardware for information literacy instruction? If so, how? Try to quantify if you can.

CHAPTER 7 – NEW TECHNOLOGIES

35. Do you use _____ to learn about new technologies?

      A.   Word of mouth
      B.   Publications
      C.   Online social networks (Twitter, Facebook, etc.)
      D.   Conferences

36. If you use another platform not listed above to learn about new technologies, please specify.

---

* Respondents to this question include only those participants who have used games or gamification concepts in IL instruction, as per Question 24

37. Are _____ a barrier or obstacle you face when trying to use new technologies in IL instruction?

    A.   Time limitations
    B.   Institutional buy-ins
    C.   Costs of equipment or software
    D.   Technical abilities

38. If there are any other barriers or obstacles you face in trying to use new technologies in IL instruction, please specify.

39. Please tell us about any other new technologies or instructional strategies that you have been using successfully in your IL instruction that were not addressed in this survey.

40. Are there any technologies that you have tried using for IL instruction that were not successful?

41. If yes, please explain.

SURVEY PARTICIPANTS

Arkansas Tech University
Aston University
Austin Peay State University
Bergen Community College
Bow Valley College
Brenau University
Bridge Valley Community and Technical College
Bronx Community College
California State University, Northridge
Carnegie Mellon University
Charter College
Chattanooga State Community College
Colgate University
College of the Holy Cross
Concordia University Irvine
DeVry University
Emporia State University
Florida Atlantic University
Globe University
Holy Names University
Hong Kong University of Science & Technology
Idaho State University
Illinois Institute of Technology
Iona College
Iowa State University
Kent State University
Lakeland College
Loyola Marymount University
Mercer County Community College
Miles Community College
Naugatuck Valley Community College
Norland College
Northeastern Illinois University
Penn State University
The Petroleum Institute
Potomac State College of West Virginia University
Renton Technical College
Rio Hondo College
Roger Williams University
Rosemont College
Saint Mary's College of California
Schoolcraft College
South University

Southern State Community College
Spartanburg Methodist College
Staffordshire University
Sul Ross State University
Tallahassee Community College
University of Connecticut
University of Illinois Springfield
University of Nebraska-Lincoln
University of North Texas
University of Oregon
University of Saint Joseph
University of Salford
The University of Scranton
University of Tennessee
University of the Incarnate Word
University of Ulster
University of Vermont
Western Michigan University
Wilmington College
Wisconsin Lutheran College

CHARACTERISTICS OF THE SAMPLE
Overall sample size: 63

By Public or Private Status
Public	38
Private	25

By Annual Full-Time Tuition
Less than $5,000	18
$5,000 to $9,999	10
$10,000 to $24,999	17
$25,000 or more	18

By Type of College
Community college	17
4-year college	14
MA-/PhD-granting college	15
Research university	17

By Full-Time Enrollment
Less than 3,000	19
3,000 to 9,999	21
10,000 or more	23

By Age of Participant
Under 40	23
40 to 49	18
50 and over	22

Public or private status of the college, broken out by annual full-time tuition prior to any deductions.

Public or Private	Less than $5,000	$5,000 to $9,999	$10,000 to $24,999	$25,000 or more
Public	47.37%	21.05%	31.58%	0.00%
Private	0.00%	8.00%	20.00%	72.00%

Public or private status of the college, broken out by type of college.

Public or Private	Community college	4-year college	MA-/PhD-granting college	Research university
Public	36.84%	13.16%	10.53%	39.47%
Private	12.00%	36.00%	44.00%	8.00%

Public or private status of the college, broken out by full-time equivalent enrollment of the college.

Public or Private	Less than 3,000	3,000 to 9,999	10,000 or more
Public	13.16%	31.58%	55.26%
Private	56.00%	36.00%	8.00%

Public or private status of the college, broken out by age of participant.

Public or Private	Under 40	40 to 49	50 and over
Public	26.32%	39.47%	34.21%
Private	52.00%	12.00%	36.00%

Annual full-time tuition prior to any deductions, broken out by public or private status of the college.

Tuition	Public	Private
Less than $5,000	100.00%	0.00%
$5,000 to $9,999	80.00%	20.00%
$10,000 to $24,999	70.59%	29.41%
$25,000 or more	0.00%	100.00%

Annual full-time tuition prior to any deductions, broken out by type of college.

Tuition	Community college	4-year college	MA-/PhD-granting college	Research university
Less than $5,000	66.67%	22.22%	0.00%	11.11%
$5,000 to $9,999	20.00%	10.00%	20.00%	50.00%
$10,000 to $24,999	11.76%	11.76%	29.41%	47.06%
$25,000 or more	5.56%	38.89%	44.44%	11.11%

Annual full-time tuition prior to any deductions, broken out by full-time equivalent enrollment of the college.

Tuition	Less than 3,000	3,000 to 9,999	10,000 or more
Less than $5,000	27.78%	50.00%	22.22%
$5,000 to $9,999	20.00%	20.00%	60.00%
$10,000 to $24,999	29.41%	5.88%	64.71%
$25,000 or more	38.89%	50.00%	11.11%

Annual full-time tuition prior to any deductions, broken out by age of participant.

Tuition	Under 40	40 to 49	50 and over
Less than $5,000	44.44%	22.22%	33.33%
$5,000 to $9,999	20.00%	40.00%	40.00%
$10,000 to $24,999	23.53%	47.06%	29.41%
$25,000 or more	50.00%	11.11%	38.89%

Type of college, broken out by public or private status of the college.

Type of College	Public	Private
Community college	82.35%	17.65%
4-year college	35.71%	64.29%
MA-/PhD-granting college	26.67%	73.33%
Research university	88.24%	11.76%

Type of college, broken out by annual full-time tuition prior to any deductions.

Type of College	Less than $5,000	$5,000 to $9,999	$10,000 to $24,999	$25,000 or more
Community college	70.59%	11.76%	11.76%	5.88%
4-year college	28.57%	7.14%	14.29%	50.00%
MA-/PhD-granting college	0.00%	13.33%	33.33%	53.33%
Research university	11.76%	29.41%	47.06%	11.76%

Type of college, broken out by full-time equivalent enrollment of the college.

Type of College	Less than 3,000	3,000 to 9,999	10,000 or more
Community college	35.29%	47.06%	17.65%
4-year college	57.14%	42.86%	0.00%
MA-/PhD-granting college	33.33%	40.00%	26.67%
Research university	0.00%	5.88%	94.12%

Type of college, broken out by age of participant.

Type of College	Under 40	40 to 49	50 and over
Community college	52.94%	17.65%	29.41%
4-year college	35.71%	28.57%	35.71%
MA-/PhD-granting college	46.67%	6.67%	46.67%
Research university	11.76%	58.82%	29.41%

Full-time equivalent enrollment of the college, broken out by public or private status of the college.

Enrollment	Public	Private
Less than 3,000	26.32%	73.68%
3,000 to 9,999	57.14%	42.86%
10,000 or more	91.30%	8.70%

Full-time equivalent enrollment of the college, broken out by annual full-time tuition prior to any deductions.

Enrollment	Less than $5,000	$5,000 to $9,999	$10,000 to $24,999	$25,000 or more
Less than 3,000	26.32%	10.53%	26.32%	36.84%
3,000 to 9,999	42.86%	9.52%	4.76%	42.86%
10,000 or more	17.39%	26.09%	47.83%	8.70%

Full-time equivalent enrollment of the college, broken out by type of college.

Enrollment	Community college	4-year college	MA-/PhD-granting college	Research university
Less than 3,000	31.58%	42.11%	26.32%	0.00%
3,000 to 9,999	38.10%	28.57%	28.57%	4.76%
10,000 or more	13.04%	0.00%	17.39%	69.57%

Full-time equivalent enrollment of the college, broken out by age of participant.

Enrollment	Under 40	40 to 49	50 and over
Less than 3,000	57.89%	5.26%	36.84%
3,000 to 9,999	42.86%	23.81%	33.33%
10,000 or more	13.04%	52.17%	34.78%

Age of participant, broken out by public or private status of the college.

Age Range	Public	Private
Under 40	43.48%	56.52%
40 to 49	83.33%	16.67%
50 and over	59.09%	40.91%

Age of participant, broken out by annual full-time tuition prior to any deductions.

Age Range	Less than $5,000	$5,000 to $9,999	$10,000 to $24,999	$25,000 or more
Under 40	34.78%	8.70%	17.39%	39.13%
40 to 49	22.22%	22.22%	44.44%	11.11%
50 and over	27.27%	18.18%	22.73%	31.82%

Age of participant, broken out by type of college.

Age Range	Community college	4-year college	MA-/PhD-granting college	Research university
Under 40	39.13%	21.74%	30.43%	8.70%
40 to 49	16.67%	22.22%	5.56%	55.56%
50 and over	22.73%	22.73%	31.82%	22.73%

Age of participant, broken out by full-time equivalent enrollment of the college.

Age Range	Less than 3,000	3,000 to 9,999	10,000 or more
Under 40	47.83%	39.13%	13.04%
40 to 49	5.56%	27.78%	66.67%
50 and over	31.82%	31.82%	36.36%

SUMMARY OF MAIN FINDINGS

Introduction

Many librarians and libraries are early adopters of new technologies and emerging pedagogical practices. These innovators provide crucial information to those either unable or less inclined to incorporate change, ultimately helping to identify new instructional strategies and tools that work, developing best practices that will allow others to bypass common mistakes, and, just as importantly, offering reliable criticism on the technologies that aren't ideal for the profession.

This report asked librarians from all levels of higher education to provide information on what new tools and instructional practices they have begun to use. The study looks at information literacy technologies in general, and then more closely examines librarians' experiences with blended learning, classroom response systems, programming and writing code, games and gamification, and mobile technologies. Thoughts and feedback are given regarding questions such as: Briefly describe a successful blended learning IL instruction experience you have had. Does your library currently use classroom response systems in any of your IL classes? What advice would you give to other librarians interested in using games for IL instruction? How has your college used tablet computers, smartphones, and other mobile computing technologies in your IL efforts?

Demographics of Sample

Individuals representing 63 higher education institutions responded, 38 (60.32%) of which were public, and 25 (39.68%) private. Types of institutions represented were mixed, with 17 (26.98%) of respondents from community colleges, 14 (22.22%) from 4-year colleges, 15 (23.81%) from MA/PhD-granting colleges, and 17 (26.98%) from research universities. Participation came from institutions with a considerably varied student full-time enrollment (FTE), with 19 (30.16%) having less than 3,000 FTE, 21 (33.33%) having between 3,000 and 9,999, and 23 (36.51%) having 10,000 or more FTE. The age of participants was also widespread, with 23 (36.51%) of respondents reporting being under 40, 18 (28.57%) between 40 and 49, and 22 (34.92%) age 50 and over.

Staff and IL Instruction

The number of employees reported to be involved in providing information literacy (IL) instruction or creating IL instruction materials varied. The largest percentage of respondents (34.92%) reported between 6 and 10 employees being involved, where institutions with less than 3,000 FTE reported either only 1 employee (42.11%) or 2-5 employees (47.37%) being involved. Conversely, of institutions with 10,000 or more FTE, 39.13% had 6 - 10 employees, and 52.17% had more than 10 employees participating in the IL instruction process.

IL Instruction Experience

The largest percentage of respondents (46.03%) reported having more than 10 years of experience providing IL instruction. Only 12.70% reported having less than 3 years of experience. The majority of respondents aged 50 and over had more than 10 years' experience (81.82%). Of respondents under 40, 43.48% had between 3 and 5 years' experience, and 30.43% had less than 3 years.

IL Instruction Delivery

The entire sample (100%) reported providing face-to-face IL instruction. A majority of respondents (66.67%) also provided online IL instruction, with 33.33% reporting not providing online IL instruction. Respondents aged 50 and over were the largest group providing online instruction (81.82%), with 40 to 49 year-olds the next largest (72.22%), and those under 40 being least likely (47.83%). Approximately half of the sample (50.79%) reported providing a hybrid of face-to-face and online IL instruction, with institutions having 10,000 or more FTE being the largest group (69.57%) to offer hybrid IL instruction.

Chapter 1 - Information Literacy Instruction Technologies

Simple Animations in IL Instruction

When asked if they had created any simple animations (such as GIFs or cartoons) for IL instruction, 25.40% responded with Yes, 38.10% stated No, but I'm interested and hope to soon, 20.63% stated No, I'm not interested, and 14.29% reported being unfamiliar with this practice. 19.05% of respondents reported having a favorite software for developing IL animations. These included Camtasia (3 mentions), PowerPoint (2 mentions), Captivate (3 mentions), Jing, GoAnimate.com (2 mentions), PowToon, SnagIt, Jing, and BrainShark.

Image Searching in IL Instruction

Image searching was being used or introduced in IL instruction by 33.33% of participants. Another 31.75% were planning on using image searching, where 12.70% were not interested, and 20.63% were not familiar with this practice. Those under 40 were the most likely to be using image searching (47.83%), where only 27.78% of 40 to 49 year-olds and 22.73% of those 50 and over used this in their instruction.

Map Searching in IL Instruction

Map searching was a less popular in IL instruction. Only 12.70% of participants stated they used maps. While 30.16% expressed interest and hoped to soon, the same percentage (30.16%) stated they were not interested, and 25.40% were not familiar with the practice. Community college librarians were the largest group using maps in IL instruction (29.41%), where less than 8% of the other three institutional types using maps. An equal number of community college librarians were also unfamiliar with using maps in IL (29.41%).

QR Codes in IL Instruction

When combined, over half of all respondents reported either using QR codes (28.57%) in IL instruction, or being interested and hoping to use them in the future (30.16%). However, 30.16% reported not being interested, and 11.11% were not familiar with QR codes. Institutions with 10,000 or more FTE were the largest group using QR codes (43.48%).

Video Searching in IL Instruction

Video searching was also a popular component of many librarians' IL instruction, with 28.57% using it and 31.75% hoping to soon. 22.22% stated that they were not interested, and 15.87% were unfamiliar with the concept. Again, community college librarians were the most likely to be using video searching (52.94%).

Video Command Searching in IL Instruction

Video command searching was only being used by 3.17% of respondents, with 38.10% being interested, 30.16% not being interested, and 26.98% being unfamiliar with the practice.

Mobile Apps for IL Instruction

When asked "Are there any mobile apps that you like for information literacy?" twenty-three participants responded. Thirteen of the responses indicated no, with at least one reason for not using apps being given as "service for polls and wireless can be spotty in some classroom locations." Of the remaining ten responses providing information on mobile apps, they listed the following: Doceri, Haiku Deck, Twitter, Facebook, Instagram (2 mentions), Pinterest, EasyBib, SMILE by Caledonian University, Flickr, ASKapp, Socrative, Google+ Hangout, Google Docs/Drive, BrainShark, YouTube, EndNote, iMovie, Simplemind. Two responses indicated using apps created in-house, such as a directional app for finding items in the building. One respondent qualified their use of social networks as a "means to examine our own information processes and behaviors."

Chapter 2 - Blended Learning and "Flipped" Classrooms

This section of questions specifically looked at the popular blended learning strategy often referred to as "flipping." In a flipped classroom, students generally prepare for class by viewing or reading lecture content, and then use class time to complete homework assignments or work through more challenging issues with assistance and interaction from a teacher.

Experience with Blended Learning Techniques

The majority of respondents (65.08%) reported using blended learning techniques in IL instruction, with another 31.75% hoping to use the practice soon. Only 1.59% of respondents were not interested, and another 1.59% unfamiliar.

Assessing Blended Learning

Assessment methodologies for blended learning practices varied. Overall, only 36.59% of those who had used blended learning used a formal assessment method to evaluate its success. This was not true for all institutions, as 72.73% of those from institutions with FTE of between 3,000 and 9,999 did indicate using formal assessment. Additionally, 58.33% of participants under the age of 40 reported using formal assessment methods, compared to 30.77% of 40 to 49 year-olds, and only 25.00% of those 50 and over. Participants were more likely to have conducted Informal assessment (63.41%) or relied on student feedback (70.73%) to determine success. Only a small percentage, 19.51, reported relying on a general feeling that it seemed "like it went well" to gauge success.

When asked to describe additional methods for determining the success of blended learning instruction experiences, nine participants provided feedback. Three of the responses indicated they were using formal assessment procedures ("Students in the flipped sessions scored about 20 points higher on the post-test administered at the semester's end" and "Course evaluations and post and pre-test analysis of student learning outcomes") and four others detailed more informal processes ("Faculty gave it high marks," "We used a SurveyMonkey for assessment"). One participant explained they were "working on integrating formal assessment this year" and another stated "There's an assumption" regarding success.

Blended Learning Environments

More participants reported using blended learning techniques in face-to-face instruction (70.73%) than online (29.27%), but this varied by age group. Face-to-face blended learning techniques decreased in popularity based on age, with 91.67% of under 40, 76.92% of 40 to 49 year-olds, and 50.00% of those 50 and over. On the other hand, use of online blended learning techniques increased by age group, with 8.33% of those under 40, 30.77% of 40 to 49 year-olds, and 43.75% of those 50 and over. Hybrid blended learning techniques had also only been used by 29.27% of participants, and showed a smaller increase in popularity by age: 16.67% of under 40, 30.77% of 40 to 49 year-olds, and 37.50% of 50 and over.

Describing Successful Blended Learning Experiences

When asked to briefly describe a successful blended learning IL instruction experience, thirty-five participants provided feedback. A number of respondents indicated having students complete worksheets prior to coming to class ("Our freshman ENG comp classes have an online module that students complete on their own with worksheets, prior to a workshop experience with their faculty and librarians"), and others had students watch videos or complete online tutorials prior to class ("I had students view two general tutorials (using our online catalog & Finding Articles) so that I could follow up on skills there and focus on what their questions were on access/mechanics so that the focus of the session could be on evaluating the sources the students find in those places."). One respondent revealed not having a successful experience, stating "Not much success. Students did not do the reading or exercises." Where nearly all of the experiences included having student's complete existing tutorials, videos, or assignments, one librarian approached the model differently: "Students were required to create the library tutorial. Each group was given a section and had to demonstrate it for the class."

Blended Learning Resources

The types of resources used in blended learning and their source of authorship varied. For those using resources created either by them or their library, the most popular was discussion questions (48.78%), followed by videos (46.34%), online tutorials (46.34%), surveys (43.90%), readings (24.39%), and pre-tests (24.39%). For those using resources created by someone else, the most popular resource was videos (26.83%), readings (21.95%), online tutorials (17.07%), surveys (9.76%), discussion questions (9.76%), and pre-tests (7.32%).

Ten participants provided information on other types of resources not mentioned. These resources included exercises, worksheets (2 mentions), online games, quizzes (2 mentions), podcasts, and a Google Calendar with "video playlist, Google Sites with links to all calendars, videos, assignments calculator schedule, and research log."

Preparation Time for Blended Learning

The amount of time spent preparing for blended learning varied. 39.02% of participants reported spending more than 1 week, 31.71% spent between 1 and 7 days, 17.07% less than 1 day, and 12.20% did not know.

Advice on Blended Learning

When asked what advice they would give to other librarians interested in using blended learning techniques, 33 participants responded. Some provided words of encouragement: "It is worth the effort!" "Keep trying!" "Learn how to do it!" "Go for it! Don't be afraid to experiment." Others expressed the need for collaborative partnerships: "Sometimes the best time to try a blended learning technique is when you're already preparing for an instruction session that happens to lend itself well to it for one reason or another - often the variable is working with a professor who is supportive of library instruction and open to trying something new;" "Have to have instructor cooperation;" "It works very well. We were able to collaborate pretty well. It takes a little while to get accustomed to team teaching;" and "Make sure you have faculty support if you plan to ask for activities to be done outside of normal class time." Finally, many shared how difficult it is: "Needs time to do right - should only use it if there are sound pedagogical reasons to do so;" "Don't be too worried if they don't do everything perfectly;" "It often takes a lot of in-class scaffolding and structure to make the lesson resonate;" "It takes much more time than I anticipated;" "Be open-minded, be willing to fail. You will learn a lot more from things that go badly than things that go well;" "Breakdown content into smaller chunks than you think necessary;" "Practice it with a small group first. It is harder than it looks and others (including faculty members) overestimate what they can do and how fast they can do it. Don't over schedule."

Chapter 3 - Classroom Response Systems

Classroom response systems, popularly known as "clickers," have been in use for a number of years. This chapter sought to find more information about who is still using these tools, what the most successful practices are, and find out why others might have turned away.

Use of Classroom Response Systems

Only 23.81% of respondents reported currently using classroom response systems. Research university librarians reported the largest percentage of use (52.94%), and community colleges the least (5.88%). Fourteen respondents provided the brand used: Turning Point (5 mentions), iClicker (4 mentions), Storify, Optivote, Near Pod, an internally developed system, and one participant could not remember the brand.

When asked what their library's plans for classroom response systems were, 28.57% responded with "Do not currently use nor do we plan to." While 9.52% reported not currently using a system, but were planning on introducing one, another 6.35% reported currently using a system but planning on using it less. 11.11% indicated no plans to change usage level, and 4.76% intended to use their system more.

Experiences with Classroom Response Systems

Twenty-nine responses were provided when prompted to "Discuss your library's experience (or your personal experience) with classroom response systems in IL instruction applications." Nine responses told of positive experiences: "It creates an environment where students are actively participating and are engaged with the content," "They are useful for some classes to generate discussion and to also gauge student's level of understanding." Eight of the responses recounted negative experiences with clickers, such as "Have experienced technical difficulties," and "A couple of librarians tried them out and then abandoned the idea. I think it took too much time to get the students up to speed since we have limited time with students." Five of the responses suggested that clicker technologies have become obsolete: "They are OK but being replaced by social media;" "Clickers become obsolete (in my opinion) through the use of mobile devices and PCs with applications like PollAnywhere and Doceri. Which are more cost effective and just as simple to use if orchestrated property;" and "Instead, I use free online products (like PollAnywhere) that utilize student's phones, since basically everyone has one." The remaining responses were from participants whose libraries were not using clickers, with at least two participants stating lack of funds as the main deterrent.

Chapter 4 - Writing Code for Information Literacy

This short chapter was looking for instances of unique or particularly effective uses of computer codes or routines for IL applications. From the limited number of responses it is apparent that very few of the survey participants were writing code to support IL instruction. Only six responses were gathered, and only two of those confirmed their libraries were doing this. One participant stated "We have several self-help learning modules for in-coming students to use to sign-up for various library services/resources," and another provided a link to an example of their library's coding work, http://www.staffs.ac.uk/ask.

Chapter 5 - Games and Gamification

Although creating entertaining assignments and competitive classroom activities are not new practices, recent developments in digital games and a broader understanding of gamification's pedagogical benefits have increased the use of games among many librarians. This chapter asked participants to describe their experiences with developing and using games and game strategies in IL instruction.

Use of Games and Gamification in IL

Just under half of participants (44.44%) had experience with using games or gamification concepts in their IL instruction. Another 44.44% hoped to begin using games soon, while 7.94% stated they were not interested, and 3.17% were not familiar with the concepts. Face-to-face games developed in-house had been used by

60.71% of participants, with 100% of those under the age of 40 reporting experience in this area. Only 21.43% of participants reported having used games developed by other libraries, and 10.71% by other non-library organizations, in face-to-face situations.

Only 17.86% reporting having created and used online games or gamification concepts. 21.43% of participants had used games developed by another library, and 0.00% of participants reported having used games developed by non-library organizations for online instruction.

Evaluating Games

When evaluating the success of their gaming activities, the majority of participants (60.71%) reported using positive student feedback. 35.71% of participants relied on a feeling that it seemed to go well, 32.14% used informal assessment, and only 17.86% formal assessment.

Advanced Skills Required for Game Development

In order to develop the games used for instruction, 32.14% reported the need for advanced skills or software. Seven respondents listed the following tools as necessary: Articulate Storyline, Captivate, Flash, Haiku Deck, HotPotatoes, Open Badges, PowerPoint, and Quia. One respondent stated that programming and video development skills were required.

Time for Development

The largest number of participants (32.14%) reported taking between 1-7 days for game development. 17.86% reported less than 1 day, and 17.86% more than 1 week. 32.14% did not know how much time development took.

Successful Game Activities in IL

Twenty-seven participants described successful experiences in using games or gamification concepts for IL instruction. Some games were simple, requiring limited tools ("Boolean searching fridge magnet game" or pen and paper scavenger hunts). Two participants reported having students use the Goblin Threat Plagiarism Game, developed by Lycoming College. Other tools mentioned included Jeopardy, The Game of Research by UT Chattanooga, and Purdue Passport Digital Badges.

Six participants provided more detailed descriptions of their gaming activities:

- ☐ We have created a quiz in which cartoon scenarios show on the screen and students use the clickers (on a timer) to submit answers and see who gets it right the fastest.

- ☐ I use a game called "The Biggest Researcher" where the goal is to find the most relevant articles on their topic. I find that instead of giving students a topic I ask them to search on their own topic so that they leave with something that they can use in their paper. We talk about the evaluation portion - how did they determine the article was going to be valuable to their paper.

- ☐ We have a matching game for understanding citation; we have a "Who Wants to be a Millionaire" type game to help students learn more about the Library and its policies (which had an unexpected use of being a very good training tool for student helpers).

- ☐ A "search off" race between individuals who look for a website featuring specific criteria and information. Encourages application of advanced search techniques.

- ☐ In class we have students get into teams and play the online game that I created. This game has students answer questions about a given source (is this peer-reviewed, who are the authors, when was it published, is it primary or secondary, etc.) to help them evaluate it. The teams get more points if they answer the questions correctly the first time. Faculty generally give the winning team extra credit points. After the game is finished we discuss the questions they had to answer in an in depth way and why those questions are useful when evaluating information.

- ☐ I used a citation game. Several MLA citations were chosen: article, book, web source. Each citation was broken down into components and written on index cards. In class, students were broken up into groups and give sets of cards. Each group had to reassemble a citation. The group to finish first puts up their citation and the class decides if it is correct or not.

Advice to Librarians Interested in Using Games

Eighteen participants provided advice to other librarians interested in using games for IL instruction. The advice ranged from encouraging ("Don't be afraid to try") to cautious ("This can also be a landmine"). Those who might be interested were told to be familiar with game design, test and retest ("Make sure that the game works on various OSs. Make sure that the game works in various browsers"), give clear instructions to students ("Make sure that student's fully grasp any directions before beginning" and "Make sure that you give students instruction in how to play and what 'winning' is"), consider using low-tech games, and know your students ("Competition does seem to drive learning for many, but leaves slower students behind. Don't make it more work for yourself than it has to be."). One participant stated the importance of using relevant concepts: "Make sure that when using activities/games that they are relevant. I tried a game one semester based on Twitter and at the time we didn't have enough Twitter users (understanding of hash tags/descriptors/subject headings) to play the game effectively. I have used the game again now that there are more Twitter users or those that at least understand the hash tag system."

Chapter 6 - Mobile Technology

As more students continue to come to campus with smartphones, mobile technologies become more prominent, and more relevant, to library instruction. This chapter sought to discover the practices and experiences librarians have with regard to mobile technologies in the classroom.

Using Mobile Computing Technologies in IL Instruction

Sixteen participants provided feedback to the question, "How has your college used tablet computers, smartphones, and other mobile computing technologies in your information literacy efforts?" Four of the responses stated they were not using mobile technologies, although one of these participants said they "do direct students to mobile apps from library vendors such as Ebrary." Of those who were using mobile technologies, the following devices were used to provide orientations, tours, scavenger hunts, IL instruction, and roaming support: iPads (4 mentions), smartphones (2 mentions), QR codes (2 mentions), Chrome books, Poll Everywhere, tablet computers, PhotoComic software, and BrowZine.

Mobile Technologies and Impact on IT Purchasing

Participants were asked to assess whether the increasing popularity of mobile computing devices had significantly impacted hardware purchasing plans regarding IL instruction. Nineteen participants responded, ten of which said there had been no changes. One response attributed the lack of change to their institution being "not interested in mobile technology." Another blamed budget cuts, "We are in our second year of budget cuts, so we don't have much money to add them. We've had to strip them out of the budget." Yet another stated their college was providing "tablets to all students and the staff get access to educational apps as part of the education budget."

Of the nine who stated purchasing decisions had changed, the amount of change ranged from "somewhat" to "most definitely." One respondent mentioned the difficulty of purchasing traditional devices and new: "Demand for desktop computers has not decreased as anticipated in the literature; demand for circulating iPads etc. remains high." Another stressed that "Library staff will need more experience with these technologies so we can know how to best use them and how our students are using them."

Chapter 7 – Other New Technologies

With so many new tools and devices appearing on the market at such a rapid pace, it is difficult, if not impossible, to predict which ones will be widely used in libraries. The final chapter allowed participants to detail what other new (or new to them) technologies they were using, and how they stay up to date with constant change.

Learning About New Technologies

With 85.71% of participants listing them as a way to learn about new technologies, conference attendance was the most popular. Word of mouth was the second most popular, at 80.95%. 76.19% of participants learned about new technologies through listservs, with 100% of community college participants using them. Publications came next, with 68.25%. Social networks were only used for this purpose by 50.79% of participants, but they were more popular among those under 40 (73.91%), compared to 55.56% of those 40 to 49, and only 22.73% of those 50 and over.

Five participants provided information on additional platforms used for learning about new technologies. These included: students, "young/tech savvy librarians," student employees, InfoToday and InfoDocket Research Buzz, research, and the IDT online masters program.

Barriers to Learning to use New Technologies

Time limitations were listed as a hurdle to learning to use new technologies by 77.78% of participants. Cost was second highest at 73.02%, followed by institutional buy-in (47.62%), and technical abilities (46.03%).

Seven respondents cited the following additional barriers: Librarian buy-in ("not sure if that is included in "institutional buy-in" but I think the institution is sometimes more ready to use new technologies than the library teachers"), technical barriers; collaborator buy-in (2 mentions) ("Need faculty buy-in for assigning 'flipped' materials before class, which can be difficult to get"); and pre-purchase evaluations ("How to make sure we have a plan for using them effectively before making the purchase, that it won't just be trendy with no positive learning outcomes").

Successful New Technologies for IL Instruction

Fifteen participants provided information on other new technologies or instructional strategies they had used successfully for IL instruction. Specific tools that were being used included: Blackboard Learn, Camtasia, Captivate, ClickShare, Credo IL Course Modules, Elluminate, Guide on the Side, Jing, LibGuides, Panopto, PollEverywhere (2 mentions), Screencast-O-Matic, and Snag-It.

Three participants provided more detailed accounts of their instructional activities:

☐ Not sure if this counts -- I have created an activity where students are asked to work in groups to evaluate resources for scholarly vs. non scholarly and then use PollEverywhere to share their analysis with the class in real time. This was a class already given iPads on a special institutional grant.

☐ The goal of the advanced comp class is to write a research paper on a topic of the student's choosing. We have found this to be successful as the students are interested in the topic they are writing about. We also have our students present the finding of their research paper through a brief presentation incorporating a multimedia resource video or music that relates to their topic. This has worked very well and we have gotten a nice response from the students.

☐ I teach mostly media literacy workshops and specifically do workshops based on projects classes are doing. I have been finding that giving students the chance to critique each other's work is very helpful - I find they often will share insights or technology skills with each other during those times.

Unsuccessful Experiences with Technologies

The final question asked participants whether they had ever had any unsuccessful experiences with using technology for IL instruction. Only 14.29% answered Yes, and 52.38% No. Ten participants provided more information. Two participants mentioned clickers ("Cumbersome, clumsy, unreliable system"), one Smart Boards and mobile tablets, and two others had difficulties when using Worlde, KnightCite, and PollEverywhere.

Four responses were especially detailed as to why their experiences weren't successful:

☐ They're all unsuccessful to *some* extent...the point is to iterate on them and figure out how they work best for you and your institution. Sometimes flipping the classroom results in the students not doing the homework beforehand if you don't have 100% faculty buy-in, and then those students have to catch up to the rest. Some of our databases don't work on the iPads.

- My videos aren't always successful. I'm getting better, but it's still a learning process.

- I tried for 3 terms to have students bring readings/text to class using their devices and found that it didn't really work. This term, I brought in (literally) reams of paper and thought the class was much more engaged and on task. (sigh)

- Quite a while back I was concerned with people ignoring instruction and going on Facebook and such during classes. I tried doing things like controlling screens or locking screens with remote desktop application and then unlocking when the time came for practice but it was cumbersome and difficult to manage while teaching - I've since dropped it and rely on GAs or instructors to monitor students and go at it with the understanding that if the student really wants to ignore the instruction and play on the laptop they are going to.

Chapter 1 – Information Literacy Instruction Technologies

Table 1 Approximately how many employees at your library provide information literacy instruction or create IL instructional materials?

Table 1.1.1 Approximately how many employees at your library provide information literacy instruction or create IL instructional materials?

	1 employee	2-5 employees	6-10 employees	More than 10 employees
Entire sample	17.46%	23.81%	34.92%	23.81%

Table 1.1.2 Approximately how many employees at your library provide information literacy instruction or create IL instructional materials? Broken out by public or private status of the college.

Public or Private	1 employee	2-5 employees	6-10 employees	More than 10 employees
Public	15.79%	15.79%	36.84%	31.58%
Private	20.00%	36.00%	32.00%	12.00%

Table 1.1.3 Approximately how many employees at your library provide information literacy instruction or create IL instructional materials? Broken out by annual full-time tuition prior to any deductions.

Tuition	1 employee	2-5 employees	6-10 employees	More than 10 employees
Less than $5,000	33.33%	22.22%	38.89%	5.56%
$5,000 to $9,999	20.00%	10.00%	30.00%	40.00%
$10,000 to $24,999	11.76%	23.53%	23.53%	41.18%
$25,000 or more	5.56%	33.33%	44.44%	16.67%

Table 1.1.4 Approximately how many employees at your library provide information literacy instruction or create IL instructional materials? Broken out by type of college.

Type of College	1 employee	2-5 employees	6-10 employees	More than 10 employees
Community college	29.41%	35.29%	29.41%	5.88%
Research university	35.71%	21.43%	28.57%	14.29%
MA-/PhD- granting college	6.67%	40.00%	33.33%	20.00%
Research university	0.00%	0.00%	47.06%	52.94%

Table 1.1.5 Approximately how many employees at your library provide information literacy instruction or create IL instructional materials? Broken out by full-time equivalent enrollment of the college.

Enrollment	1 employee	2-5 employees	6-10 employees	More than 10 employees
Less than 3,000	42.11%	47.37%	10.53%	0.00%
10,000 or more	9.52%	23.81%	52.38%	14.29%
10,000 or more	4.35%	4.35%	39.13%	52.17%

Table 1.1.6 Approximately how many employees at your library provide information literacy instruction or create IL instructional materials? Broken out by age of participant.

Age Range	1 employee	2-5 employees	6-10 employees	More than 10 employees
Under 40	26.09%	30.43%	30.43%	13.04%
40 to 49	11.11%	5.56%	38.89%	44.44%
50 and over	13.64%	31.82%	36.36%	18.18%

Table 2 Approximately how long have you been providing and/or creating information literacy instruction?

Table 2.1.1 Approximately how long have you been providing and/or creating information literacy instruction?

	Less than 3 years	3-5 years	6-10 years	More than 10 years
Entire sample	12.70%	20.63%	20.63%	46.03%

Table 2.1.2 Approximately how long have you been providing and/or creating information literacy instruction? Broken out by public or private status of the college.

Public or Private	Less than 3 years	3-5 years	6-10 years	More than 10 years
Public	10.53%	15.79%	15.79%	57.89%
Private	16.00%	28.00%	28.00%	28.00%

Table 2.1.3 Approximately how long have you been providing and/or creating information literacy instruction? Broken out by annual full-time tuition prior to any deductions.

Tuition	Less than 3 years	3-5 years	6-10 years	More than 10 years
Less than $5,000	16.67%	27.78%	16.67%	38.89%
$5,000 to $9,999	10.00%	10.00%	10.00%	70.00%
$10,000 to $24,999	5.88%	5.88%	35.29%	52.94%
$25,000 or more	16.67%	33.33%	16.67%	33.33%

Table 2.1.4 Approximately how long have you been providing and/or creating information literacy instruction? Broken out by type of college.

Type of College	Less than 3 years	3-5 years	6-10 years	More than 10 years
Community college	17.65%	29.41%	17.65%	35.29%
Research university	21.43%	21.43%	21.43%	35.71%
MA-/PhD-granting college	13.33%	26.67%	20.00%	40.00%
Research university	0.00%	5.88%	23.53%	70.59%

Table 2.1.5 Approximately how long have you been providing and/or creating information literacy instruction? Broken out by full-time equivalent enrollment of the college.

Enrollment	Less than 3 years	3-5 years	6-10 years	More than 10 years
Less than 3,000	10.53%	31.58%	21.05%	36.84%
10,000 or more	23.81%	23.81%	23.81%	28.57%
10,000 or more	4.35%	8.70%	17.39%	69.57%

Table 2.1.6 Approximately how long have you been providing and/or creating information literacy instruction? Broken out by age of participant.

Age Range	Less than 3 years	3-5 years	6-10 years	More than 10 years
Under 40	30.43%	43.48%	21.74%	4.35%
40 to 49	5.56%	5.56%	33.33%	55.56%
50 and over	0.00%	9.09%	9.09%	81.82%

Table 3 Do you provide face-to-face IL instruction?

Table 3.1.1 Do you provide face-to-face IL instruction?

	No Answer	Yes	No
Entire sample	0.00%	100.00%	0.00%

Table 4 Do you provide online IL instruction?

Table 4.1.1 Do you provide online IL instruction?

	No Answer	Yes	No
Entire sample	0.00%	66.67%	33.33%

Table 4.1.2 Do you provide online IL instruction? Broken out by public or private status of the college.

Public or Private	Yes	No
Public	73.68%	26.32%
Private	56.00%	44.00%

Table 4.1.3 Do you provide online IL instruction? Broken out by annual full-time tuition prior to any deductions.

Tuition	Yes	No
Less than $5,000	72.22%	27.78%
$5,000 to $9,999	70.00%	30.00%
$10,000 to $24,999	76.47%	23.53%
$25,000 or more	50.00%	50.00%

Table 4.1.4 Do you provide online IL instruction? Broken out by type of college.

Type of College	Yes	No
Community college	70.59%	29.41%
Research university	57.14%	42.86%
MA-/PhD-granting college	66.67%	33.33%
Research university	70.59%	29.41%

Table 4.1.5 Do you provide online IL instruction? Broken out by full-time equivalent enrollment of the college.

Enrollment	Yes	No
Less than 3,000	63.16%	36.84%
10,000 or more	61.90%	38.10%
10,000 or more	73.91%	26.09%

Table 4.1.6 Do you provide online IL instruction? Broken out by age of participant.

Age Range	Yes	No
Under 40	47.83%	52.17%
40 to 49	72.22%	27.78%
50 and over	81.82%	18.18%

Table 5 Do you provide hybrid (face-to-face and online) IL instruction?

Table 5.1.1 Do you provide hybrid (face-to-face and online) IL instruction?

	No Answer	Yes	No
Entire sample	0.00%	50.79%	49.21%

Table 5.1.2 Do you provide hybrid (face-to-face and online) IL instruction? Broken out by public or private status of the college.

Public or Private	Yes	No
Public	65.79%	34.21%
Private	28.00%	72.00%

Table 5.1.3 Do you provide hybrid (face-to-face and online) IL instruction? Broken out by annual full-time tuition prior to any deductions.

Tuition	Yes	No
Less than $5,000	55.56%	44.44%
$5,000 to $9,999	50.00%	50.00%
$10,000 to $24,999	76.47%	23.53%
$25,000 or more	22.22%	77.78%

Table 5.1.4 Do you provide hybrid (face-to-face and online) IL instruction? Broken out by type of college.

Type of College	Yes	No
Community college	47.06%	52.94%
Research university	35.71%	64.29%
MA-/PhD-granting college	46.67%	53.33%
Research university	70.59%	29.41%

Table 5.1.5 Do you provide hybrid (face-to-face and online) IL instruction? Broken out by full-time equivalent enrollment of the college.

Enrollment	Yes	No
Less than 3,000	47.37%	52.63%
10,000 or more	33.33%	66.67%
10,000 or more	69.57%	30.43%

Table 5.1.6 Do you provide hybrid (face-to-face and online) IL instruction? Broken out by age of participant.

Age Range	Yes	No
Under 40	30.43%	69.57%
40 to 49	50.00%	50.00%
50 and over	72.73%	27.27%

Table 6 Have you created any simple animations (such as GIFs or cartoons) for your IL instruction?

Table 6.1.1 Have you created any simple animations (such as GIFs or cartoons) for your IL instruction?

	No Answer	Yes	No, but I'm interested and hope to soon	No, I'm not interested	No, I'm not familiar with this
Entire sample	1.59%	25.40%	38.10%	20.63%	14.29%

Table 6.1.2 Have you created any simple animations (such as GIFs or cartoons) for your IL instruction? Broken out by public or private status of the college.

Public or Private	No Answer	Yes	No, but I'm interested and hope to soon	No, I'm not interested	No, I'm not familiar with this
Public	2.63%	21.05%	42.11%	18.42%	15.79%
Private	0.00%	32.00%	32.00%	24.00%	12.00%

Table 6.1.3 Have you created any simple animations (such as GIFs or cartoons) for your IL instruction? Broken out by annual full-time tuition prior to any deductions.

Tuition	No Answer	Yes	No, but I'm interested and hope to soon	No, I'm not interested	No, I'm not familiar with this
Less than $5,000	5.56%	5.56%	66.67%	16.67%	5.56%
$5,000 to $9,999	0.00%	30.00%	20.00%	20.00%	30.00%
$10,000 to $24,999	0.00%	35.29%	29.41%	11.76%	23.53%
$25,000 or more	0.00%	33.33%	27.78%	33.33%	5.56%

Table 6.1.4 Have you created any simple animations (such as GIFs or cartoons) for your IL instruction? Broken out by type of college.

Type of College	No Answer	Yes	No, but I'm interested and hope to soon	No, I'm not interested	No, I'm not familiar with this
Community college	5.88%	11.76%	64.71%	11.76%	5.88%
Research university	0.00%	21.43%	21.43%	28.57%	28.57%
MA-/PhD-granting college	0.00%	26.67%	33.33%	20.00%	20.00%
Research university	0.00%	41.18%	29.41%	23.53%	5.88%

Table 6.1.5 Have you created any simple animations (such as GIFs or cartoons) for your IL instruction? Broken out by full-time equivalent enrollment of the college.

Enrollment	No Answer	Yes	No, but I'm interested and hope to soon	No, I'm not interested	No, I'm not familiar with this
Less than 3,000	5.26%	26.32%	42.11%	10.53%	15.79%
10,000 or more	0.00%	14.29%	42.86%	33.33%	9.52%
10,000 or more	0.00%	34.78%	30.43%	17.39%	17.39%

Table 6.1.6 Have you created any simple animations (such as GIFs or cartoons) for your IL instruction? Broken out by age of participant.

Age Range	No Answer	Yes	No, but I'm interested and hope to soon	No, I'm not interested	No, I'm not familiar with this
Under 40	0.00%	17.39%	43.48%	21.74%	17.39%
40 to 49	0.00%	33.33%	33.33%	11.11%	22.22%
50 and over	4.55%	27.27%	36.36%	27.27%	4.55%

Table 7 Do you have a favorite software for developing IL animations?

Table 7.1.1 Do you have a favorite software for developing IL animations?

	No Answer	Yes	No	I'm not making IL animations
Entire sample	1.59%	19.05%	34.92%	44.44%

Table 7.1.2 Do you have a favorite software for developing IL animations? Broken out by public or private status of the college.

Public or Private	No Answer	Yes	No	I'm not making IL animations
Public	2.63%	21.05%	31.58%	44.74%
Private	0.00%	16.00%	40.00%	44.00%

Table 7.1.3 Do you have a favorite software for developing IL animations? Broken out by annual full-time tuition prior to any deductions.

Tuition	No Answer	Yes	No	I'm not making IL animations
Less than $5,000	5.56%	16.67%	27.78%	50.00%
$5,000 to $9,999	0.00%	30.00%	30.00%	40.00%
$10,000 to $24,999	0.00%	17.65%	47.06%	35.29%
$25,000 or more	0.00%	16.67%	33.33%	50.00%

Table 7.1.4 Do you have a favorite software for developing IL animations? Broken out by type of college.

Type of College	No Answer	Yes	No	I'm not making IL animations
Community college	5.88%	23.53%	41.18%	29.41%
Research university	0.00%	7.14%	14.29%	78.57%
MA-/PhD-granting college	0.00%	20.00%	46.67%	33.33%
Research university	0.00%	23.53%	35.29%	41.18%

Table 7.1.5 Do you have a favorite software for developing IL animations? Broken out by full-time equivalent enrollment of the college.

Enrollment	No Answer	Yes	No	I'm not making IL animations
Less than 3,000	5.26%	10.53%	42.11%	42.11%
10,000 or more	0.00%	23.81%	14.29%	61.90%
10,000 or more	0.00%	21.74%	47.83%	30.43%

Table 7.1.6 Do you have a favorite software for developing IL animations? Broken out by age of participant.

Age Range	No Answer	Yes	No	I'm not making IL animations
Under 40	0.00%	4.35%	43.48%	52.17%
40 to 49	0.00%	16.67%	33.33%	50.00%
50 and over	4.55%	36.36%	27.27%	31.82%

If you do have a favorite software for IL animations, what is it?

1. Camtasia, Captivate, Final Cut Pro.

2. Camtasia.

3. PowerPoint.

4. Capitivate.

5. Jing and Camtasia.

6. goanimate.com.

7. We use Captivate (mainly).

8. PowToon.

9. GoAnimate.

10. I use Adobe & Publisher for graphics. I use Captivate, Snagit, Jing, PowerPoint, and BrainShark for videos/animations.

Table 8 Are you using or introducing image searching in your IL instruction?

Table 8.1.1 Are you using or introducing image searching in your IL instruction?

	No Answer	Yes	No, but I 'm interested and hope to soon	No, I'm not interested	No, I'm not familiar with this
Entire sample	1.59%	33.33%	31.75%	12.70%	20.63%

Table 8.1.2 Are you using or introducing image searching in your IL instruction? Broken out by public or private status of the college.

Public or Private	No Answer	Yes	No, but I 'm interested and hope to soon	No, I'm not interested	No, I'm not familiar with this
Public	2.63%	31.58%	39.47%	10.53%	15.79%
Private	0.00%	36.00%	20.00%	16.00%	28.00%

Table 8.1.3 Are you using or introducing image searching in your IL instruction? Broken out by annual full-time tuition prior to any deductions.

Tuition	No Answer	Yes	No, but I 'm interested and hope to soon	No, I'm not interested	No, I'm not familiar with this
Less than $5,000	0.00%	27.78%	44.44%	5.56%	22.22%
$5,000 to $9,999	0.00%	30.00%	40.00%	10.00%	20.00%
$10,000 to $24,999	5.88%	47.06%	23.53%	17.65%	5.88%
$25,000 or more	0.00%	27.78%	22.22%	16.67%	33.33%

Table 8.1.4 Are you using or introducing image searching in your IL instruction? Broken out by type of college.

Type of College	No Answer	Yes	No, but I 'm interested and hope to soon	No, I'm not interested	No, I'm not familiar with this
Community college	0.00%	47.06%	23.53%	5.88%	23.53%
Research university	0.00%	14.29%	57.14%	0.00%	28.57%
MA-/PhD-granting college	0.00%	33.33%	13.33%	26.67%	26.67%
Research university	5.88%	35.29%	35.29%	17.65%	5.88%

Table 8.1.5 Are you using or introducing image searching in your IL instruction? Broken out by full-time equivalent enrollment of the college.

Enrollment	No Answer	Yes	No, but I 'm interested and hope to soon	No, I'm not interested	No, I'm not familiar with this
Less than 3,000	0.00%	42.11%	31.58%	5.26%	21.05%
10,000 or more	0.00%	23.81%	23.81%	23.81%	28.57%
10,000 or more	4.35%	34.78%	39.13%	8.70%	13.04%

Table 8.1.6 Are you using or introducing image searching in your IL instruction? Broken out by age of participant.

Age Range	No Answer	Yes	No, but I 'm interested and hope to soon	No, I'm not interested	No, I'm not familiar with this
Under 40	0.00%	47.83%	26.09%	13.04%	13.04%
40 to 49	5.56%	27.78%	33.33%	16.67%	16.67%
50 and over	0.00%	22.73%	36.36%	9.09%	31.82%

Table 9 Are you using or introducing map searching in your IL instruction?

Table 9.1.1 Are you using or introducing map searching in your IL instruction?

	No Answer	Yes	No, but I 'm interested and hope to soon	No, I'm not interested	No, I'm not familiar with this
Entire sample	1.59%	12.70%	30.16%	30.16%	25.40%

Table 9.1.2 Are you using or introducing map searching in your IL instruction? Broken out by public or private status of the college.

Public or Private	No Answer	Yes	No, but I 'm interested and hope to soon	No, I'm not interested	No, I'm not familiar with this
Public	2.63%	15.79%	26.32%	28.95%	26.32%
Private	0.00%	8.00%	36.00%	32.00%	24.00%

Table 9.1.3 Are you using or introducing map searching in your IL instruction? Broken out by annual full-time tuition prior to any deductions.

Tuition	No Answer	Yes	No, but I 'm interested and hope to soon	No, I'm not interested	No, I'm not familiar with this
Less than $5,000	0.00%	16.67%	27.78%	22.22%	33.33%
$5,000 to $9,999	0.00%	10.00%	20.00%	40.00%	30.00%
$10,000 to $24,999	5.88%	17.65%	23.53%	41.18%	11.76%
$25,000 or more	0.00%	5.56%	44.44%	22.22%	27.78%

Table 9.1.4 Are you using or introducing map searching in your IL instruction? Broken out by type of college.

Type of College	No Answer	Yes	No, but I 'm interested and hope to soon	No, I'm not interested	No, I'm not familiar with this
Community college	0.00%	29.41%	17.65%	23.53%	29.41%
Research university	0.00%	7.14%	42.86%	7.14%	42.86%
MA-/PhD-granting college	0.00%	6.67%	33.33%	46.67%	13.33%
Research university	5.88%	5.88%	29.41%	41.18%	17.65%

Table 9.1.5 Are you using or introducing map searching in your IL instruction? Broken out by full-time equivalent enrollment of the college.

Enrollment	No Answer	Yes	No, but I 'm interested and hope to soon	No, I'm not interested	No, I'm not familiar with this
Less than 3,000	0.00%	15.79%	26.32%	31.58%	26.32%
10,000 or more	0.00%	4.76%	33.33%	33.33%	28.57%
10,000 or more	4.35%	17.39%	30.43%	26.09%	21.74%

Table 9.1.6 Are you using or introducing map searching in your IL instruction? Broken out by age of participant.

Age Range	No Answer	Yes	No, but I 'm interested and hope to soon	No, I'm not interested	No, I'm not familiar with this
Under 40	0.00%	17.39%	39.13%	26.09%	17.39%
40 to 49	5.56%	5.56%	22.22%	33.33%	33.33%
50 and over	0.00%	13.64%	27.27%	31.82%	27.27%

Table 10 Are you using or introducing QR codes in your IL instruction?

Table 10.1.1 Are you using or introducing QR codes in your IL instruction?

	Yes	No, but I 'm interested and hope to soon	No, I'm not interested	No, I'm not familiar with this
Entire sample	28.57%	30.16%	30.16%	11.11%

Table 10.1.2 Are you using or introducing QR codes in your IL instruction? Broken out by public or private status of the college.

Public or Private	Yes	No, but I 'm interested and hope to soon	No, I'm not interested	No, I'm not familiar with this
Public	31.58%	28.95%	31.58%	7.89%
Private	24.00%	32.00%	28.00%	16.00%

Table 10.1.3 Are you using or introducing QR codes in your IL instruction? Broken out by annual full-time tuition prior to any deductions.

Tuition	Yes	No, but I 'm interested and hope to soon	No, I'm not interested	No, I'm not familiar with this
Less than $5,000	16.67%	33.33%	38.89%	11.11%
$5,000 to $9,999	30.00%	40.00%	10.00%	20.00%
$10,000 to $24,999	47.06%	17.65%	35.29%	0.00%
$25,000 or more	22.22%	33.33%	27.78%	16.67%

Table 10.1.4 Are you using or introducing QR codes in your IL instruction? Broken out by type of college.

Type of College	Yes	No, but I 'm interested and hope to soon	No, I'm not interested	No, I'm not familiar with this
Community college	29.41%	35.29%	23.53%	11.76%
Research university	21.43%	35.71%	21.43%	21.43%
MA-/PhD-granting college	26.67%	33.33%	33.33%	6.67%
Research university	35.29%	17.65%	41.18%	5.88%

Table 10.1.5 Are you using or introducing QR codes in your IL instruction? Broken out by full-time equivalent enrollment of the college.

Enrollment	Yes	No, but I 'm interested and hope to soon	No, I'm not interested	No, I'm not familiar with this
Less than 3,000	26.32%	42.11%	21.05%	10.53%
10,000 or more	14.29%	28.57%	42.86%	14.29%
10,000 or more	43.48%	21.74%	26.09%	8.70%

Table 10.1.6 Are you using or introducing QR codes in your IL instruction? Broken out by age of participant.

Age Range	Yes	No, but I 'm interested and hope to soon	No, I'm not interested	No, I'm not familiar with this
Under 40	34.78%	34.78%	26.09%	4.35%
40 to 49	33.33%	16.67%	38.89%	11.11%
50 and over	18.18%	36.36%	27.27%	18.18%

Table 11 Are you using or introducing video searching in your IL instruction?

Table 11.1.1 Are you using or introducing video searching in your IL instruction?

	No Answer	Yes	No, but I 'm interested and hope to soon	No, I'm not interested	No, I'm not familiar with this
Entire sample	1.59%	28.57%	31.75%	22.22%	15.87%

Table 11.1.2 Are you using or introducing video searching in your IL instruction? Broken out by public or private status of the college.

Public or Private	No Answer	Yes	No, but I 'm interested and hope to soon	No, I'm not interested	No, I'm not familiar with this
Public	2.63%	28.95%	28.95%	23.68%	15.79%
Private	0.00%	28.00%	36.00%	20.00%	16.00%

Table 11.1.3 Are you using or introducing video searching in your IL instruction? Broken out by annual full-time tuition prior to any deductions.

Tuition	No Answer	Yes	No, but I 'm interested and hope to soon	No, I'm not interested	No, I'm not familiar with this
Less than $5,000	0.00%	27.78%	33.33%	22.22%	16.67%
$5,000 to $9,999	0.00%	20.00%	20.00%	20.00%	40.00%
$10,000 to $24,999	5.88%	35.29%	35.29%	23.53%	0.00%
$25,000 or more	0.00%	27.78%	33.33%	22.22%	16.67%

Table 11.1.4 Are you using or introducing video searching in your IL instruction? Broken out by type of college.

Type of College	No Answer	Yes	No, but I 'm interested and hope to soon	No, I'm not interested	No, I'm not familiar with this
Community college	0.00%	52.94%	17.65%	11.76%	17.65%
Research university	0.00%	14.29%	50.00%	14.29%	21.43%
MA-/PhD- granting college	0.00%	33.33%	33.33%	26.67%	6.67%
Research university	5.88%	11.76%	29.41%	35.29%	17.65%

Table 11.1.5 Are you using or introducing video searching in your IL instruction? Broken out by full-time equivalent enrollment of the college.

Enrollment	No Answer	Yes	No, but I 'm interested and hope to soon	No, I'm not interested	No, I'm not familiar with this
Less than 3,000	0.00%	31.58%	36.84%	15.79%	15.79%
10,000 or more	0.00%	28.57%	28.57%	28.57%	14.29%
10,000 or more	4.35%	26.09%	30.43%	21.74%	17.39%

Table 11.1.6 Are you using or introducing video searching in your IL instruction? Broken out by age of participant.

Age Range	No Answer	Yes	No, but I 'm interested and hope to soon	No, I'm not interested	No, I'm not familiar with this
Under 40	0.00%	39.13%	34.78%	17.39%	8.70%
40 to 49	5.56%	11.11%	38.89%	22.22%	22.22%
50 and over	0.00%	31.82%	22.73%	27.27%	18.18%

Table 12 Are you using or introducing video command searching in your IL instruction?

Table 12.1.1 Are you using or introducing video command searching in your IL instruction?

	No Answer	Yes	No, but I 'm interested and hope to soon	No, I'm not interested	No, I'm not familiar with this
Entire sample	1.59%	3.17%	38.10%	30.16%	26.98%

Table 12.1.2 Are you using or introducing video command searching in your IL instruction? Broken out by public or private status of the college.

Public or Private	No Answer	Yes	No, but I 'm interested and hope to soon	No, I'm not interested	No, I'm not familiar with this
Public	2.63%	2.63%	44.74%	23.68%	26.32%
Private	0.00%	4.00%	28.00%	40.00%	28.00%

Table 12.1.3 Are you using or introducing video command searching in your IL instruction? Broken out by annual full-time tuition prior to any deductions.

Tuition	No Answer	Yes	No, but I 'm interested and hope to soon	No, I'm not interested	No, I'm not familiar with this
Less than $5,000	0.00%	0.00%	44.44%	16.67%	38.89%
$5,000 to $9,999	0.00%	0.00%	20.00%	40.00%	40.00%
$10,000 to $24,999	5.88%	5.88%	58.82%	23.53%	5.88%
$25,000 or more	0.00%	5.56%	22.22%	44.44%	27.78%

Table 12.1.4 Are you using or introducing video command searching in your IL instruction? Broken out by type of college.

Type of College	No Answer	Yes	No, but I 'm interested and hope to soon	No, I'm not interested	No, I'm not familiar with this
Community college	0.00%	0.00%	64.71%	5.88%	29.41%
Research university	0.00%	7.14%	21.43%	21.43%	50.00%
MA-/PhD- granting college	0.00%	0.00%	40.00%	53.33%	6.67%
Research university	5.88%	5.88%	23.53%	41.18%	23.53%

Table 12.1.5 Are you using or introducing video command searching in your IL instruction? Broken out by full-time equivalent enrollment of the college.

Enrollment	No Answer	Yes	No, but I 'm interested and hope to soon	No, I'm not interested	No, I'm not familiar with this
Less than 3,000	0.00%	5.26%	42.11%	21.05%	31.58%
10,000 or more	0.00%	0.00%	28.57%	42.86%	28.57%
10,000 or more	4.35%	4.35%	43.48%	26.09%	21.74%

Table 12.1.6 Are you using or introducing video command searching in your IL instruction? Broken out by age of participant.

Age Range	No Answer	Yes	No, but I 'm interested and hope to soon	No, I'm not interested	No, I'm not familiar with this
Under 40	0.00%	4.35%	43.48%	30.43%	21.74%
40 to 49	5.56%	5.56%	33.33%	27.78%	27.78%
50 and over	0.00%	0.00%	36.36%	31.82%	31.82%

Are there any mobile apps that you like for information literacy?

1. None that stand out.

2. Not that I'm familiar with.

3. Doceri, haiku deck.

4. Twitter, Facebook, Instagram and Pinterest (social networks as a means to examine our own information processes and behaviors).

5. I have not made mobile apps a required part of instruction.

6. Do not know enough to add it to our teaching.

7. No.

8. None used.

9. Don't know of any, haven't looked.

10. EasyBib citation app.

11. SMILE by Caledonian University.

12. Haven't used any - service for polls and wireless can be spotty in some classroom locations.

13. I don't use mobile apps.

14. Flickr.

15. Directional app for finding items in the building.

16. No.

17. No.

18. ASKapp - shortly to be released.

19. Socrative, Instagram.

20. Do you include web apps in mobile apps? I use Google+ Hangout, Google Docs/Drive, BrainShark, YouTube, and more.

21. Not at this time.

22. Do not use.

23. Endnote.

24. Our own.

25. iMovie.

26. None.

27. I use the free version of simplemind to do mindmap/brainstorming exercizes.

Chapter 2 – Blended Learning and "Flipped" Classrooms

Table 13 Have you ever used blended learning techniques in your IL instruction?

Table 13.1.1 Have you ever used blended learning techniques in your IL instruction?

	Yes	No, but I 'm interested and hope to soon	No, I'm not interested	No, I'm not familiar with this
Entire sample	65.08%	31.75%	1.59%	1.59%

Table 13.1.2 Have you ever used blended learning techniques in your IL instruction? Broken out by public or private status of the college.

Public or Private	Yes	No, but I 'm interested and hope to soon	No, I'm not interested	No, I'm not familiar with this
Public	68.42%	28.95%	2.63%	0.00%
Private	60.00%	36.00%	0.00%	4.00%

Table 13.1.3 Have you ever used blended learning techniques in your IL instruction? Broken out by annual full-time tuition prior to any deductions.

Tuition	Yes	No, but I 'm interested and hope to soon	No, I'm not interested	No, I'm not familiar with this
Less than $5,000	72.22%	22.22%	5.56%	0.00%
$5,000 to $9,999	40.00%	60.00%	0.00%	0.00%
$10,000 to $24,999	82.35%	11.76%	0.00%	5.88%
$25,000 or more	55.56%	44.44%	0.00%	0.00%

Table 13.1.4 Have you ever used blended learning techniques in your IL instruction? Broken out by type of college.

Type of College	Yes	No, but I 'm interested and hope to soon	No, I'm not interested	No, I'm not familiar with this
Community college	52.94%	35.29%	5.88%	5.88%
Research university	71.43%	28.57%	0.00%	0.00%
MA-/PhD-granting college	73.33%	26.67%	0.00%	0.00%
Research university	64.71%	35.29%	0.00%	0.00%

Table 13.1.5 Have you ever used blended learning techniques in your IL instruction? Broken out by full-time equivalent enrollment of the college.

Enrollment	Yes	No, but I 'm interested and hope to soon	No, I'm not interested	No, I'm not familiar with this
Less than 3,000	68.42%	26.32%	0.00%	5.26%
10,000 or more	52.38%	42.86%	4.76%	0.00%
10,000 or more	73.91%	26.09%	0.00%	0.00%

Table 13.1.6 Have you ever used blended learning techniques in your IL instruction? Broken out by age of participant.

Age Range	Yes	No, but I 'm interested and hope to soon	No, I'm not interested	No, I'm not familiar with this
Under 40	52.17%	43.48%	0.00%	4.35%
40 to 49	72.22%	27.78%	0.00%	0.00%
50 and over	72.73%	22.73%	4.55%	0.00%

Table 14 If you have used blended learning techniques in your IL instruction, did you determine your experience to be successful thanks to a formal assessment?[*]

Table 14.1.1 If you have used blended learning techniques in your IL instruction, did you determine your experience to be successful thanks to a formal assessment?

	Yes	No
Entire sample	36.59%	63.41%

Table 14.1.2 If you have used blended learning techniques in your IL instruction, did you determine your experience to be successful thanks to a formal assessment? Broken out by public or private status of the college.

Public or Private	Yes	No
Public	34.62%	65.38%
Private	40.00%	60.00%

Table 14.1.3 If you have used blended learning techniques in your IL instruction, did you determine your experience to be successful thanks to a formal assessment? Broken out by annual full-time tuition prior to any deductions.

Tuition	Yes	No
Less than $5,000	46.15%	53.85%
$5,000 to $9,999	50.00%	50.00%
$10,000 to $24,999	7.14%	92.86%
$25,000 or more	60.00%	40.00%

---

[*] Respondents to this question include only those participants who have used blended learning techniques in IL instruction, as per Table 13

90

Table 14.1.4 If you have used blended learning techniques in your IL instruction, did you determine your experience to be successful thanks to a formal assessment? Broken out by type of college.

Type of College	Yes	No
Community college	44.44%	55.56%
4-year college	30.00%	70.00%
MA-/PhD-granting college	45.45%	54.55%
Research university	27.27%	72.73%

Table 14.1.5 If you have used blended learning techniques in your IL instruction, did you determine your experience to be successful thanks to a formal assessment? Broken out by full-time equivalent enrollment of the college.

Enrollment	Yes	No
Less than 3,000	23.08%	76.92%
3,000 to 9,999	72.73%	27.27%
10,000 or more	23.53%	76.47%

Table 14.1.6 If you have used blended learning techniques in your IL instruction, did you determine your experience to be successful thanks to a formal assessment? Broken out by age of participant.

Age Range	Yes	No
Under 40	58.33%	41.67%
40 to 49	30.77%	69.23%
50 and over	25.00%	75.00%

Table 15 If you have used blended learning techniques in your IL instruction, did you determine your experience to be successful thanks to an informal assessment?[*]

Table 15.1.1 If you have used blended learning techniques in your IL instruction, did you determine your experience to be successful thanks to an informal assessment?

	Yes	No
Entire sample	63.41%	36.59%

Table 15.1.2 If you have used blended learning techniques in your IL instruction, did you determine your experience to be successful thanks to an informal assessment? Broken out by public or private status of the college.

Public or Private	Yes	No
Public	65.38%	34.62%
Private	60.00%	40.00%

Table 15.1.3 If you have used blended learning techniques in your IL instruction, did you determine your experience to be successful thanks to an informal assessment? Broken out by annual full-time tuition prior to any deductions.

Tuition	Yes	No
Less than $5,000	69.23%	30.77%
$5,000 to $9,999	75.00%	25.00%
$10,000 to $24,999	64.29%	35.71%
$25,000 or more	50.00%	50.00%

---

[*] Respondents to this question include only those participants who have used blended learning techniques in IL instruction, as per Table 13

Table 15.1.4 If you have used blended learning techniques in your IL instruction, did you determine your experience to be successful thanks to an informal assessment? Broken out by type of college.

Type of College	Yes	No
Community college	66.67%	33.33%
4-year college	60.00%	40.00%
MA-/PhD-granting college	45.45%	54.55%
Research university	81.82%	18.18%

Table 15.1.5 If you have used blended learning techniques in your IL instruction, did you determine your experience to be successful thanks to an informal assessment? Broken out by full-time equivalent enrollment of the college.

Enrollment	Yes	No
Less than 3,000	46.15%	53.85%
3,000 to 9,999	72.73%	27.27%
10,000 or more	70.59%	29.41%

Table 15.1.6 If you have used blended learning techniques in your IL instruction, did you determine your experience to be successful thanks to an informal assessment? Broken out by age of participant.

Age Range	Yes	No
Under 40	50.00%	50.00%
40 to 49	76.92%	23.08%
50 and over	62.50%	37.50%

Table 16 If you have used blended learning techniques in your IL instruction, did you determine your experience to be successful thanks to positive student feedback?[*]

Table 16.1.1 If you have used blended learning techniques in your IL instruction, did you determine your experience to be successful thanks to positive student feedback?

	Yes	No
Entire sample	70.73%	29.27%

Table 16.1.2 If you have used blended learning techniques in your IL instruction, did you determine your experience to be successful thanks to positive student feedback? Broken out by public or private status of the college.

Public or Private	Yes	No
Public	73.08%	26.92%
Private	66.67%	33.33%

Table 16.1.3 If you have used blended learning techniques in your IL instruction, did you determine your experience to be successful thanks to positive student feedback? Broken out by annual full-time tuition prior to any deductions.

Tuition	Yes	No
Less than $5,000	69.23%	30.77%
$5,000 to $9,999	100.00%	0.00%
$10,000 to $24,999	71.43%	28.57%
$25,000 or more	60.00%	40.00%

---

[*] Respondents to this question include only those participants who have used blended learning techniques in IL instruction, as per Table 13

Table 16.1.4 If you have used blended learning techniques in your IL instruction, did you determine your experience to be successful thanks to positive student feedback? Broken out by type of college.

Type of College	Yes	No
Community college	77.78%	22.22%
4-year college	60.00%	40.00%
MA-/PhD-granting college	63.64%	36.36%
Research university	81.82%	18.18%

Table 16.1.5 If you have used blended learning techniques in your IL instruction, did you determine your experience to be successful thanks to positive student feedback? Broken out by full-time equivalent enrollment of the college.

Enrollment	Yes	No
Less than 3,000	76.92%	23.08%
3,000 to 9,999	36.36%	63.64%
10,000 or more	88.24%	11.76%

Table 16.1.6 If you have used blended learning techniques in your IL instruction, did you determine your experience to be successful thanks to positive student feedback? Broken out by age of participant.

Age Range	Yes	No
Under 40	75.00%	25.00%
40 to 49	69.23%	30.77%
50 and over	68.75%	31.25%

Table 17 If you have used blended learning techniques in your IL instruction, did you determine your experience to be successful thanks to it seeming like it went well?[*]

Table 17.1.1 If you have used blended learning techniques in your IL instruction, did you determine your experience to be successful thanks to it seeming like it went well?

	Yes	No
Entire sample	19.51%	80.49%

Table 17.1.2 If you have used blended learning techniques in your IL instruction, did you determine your experience to be successful thanks to it seeming like it went well? Broken out by public or private status of the college.

Public or Private	Yes	No
Public	23.08%	76.92%
Private	13.33%	86.67%

Table 17.1.3 If you have used blended learning techniques in your IL instruction, did you determine your experience to be successful thanks to it seeming like it went well? Broken out by annual full-time tuition prior to any deductions.

Tuition	Yes	No
Less than $5,000	23.08%	76.92%
$5,000 to $9,999	25.00%	75.00%
$10,000 to $24,999	28.57%	71.43%
$25,000 or more	0.00%	100.00%

---

[*] Respondents to this question include only those participants who have used blended learning techniques in IL instruction, as per Table 13

Table 17.1.4 If you have used blended learning techniques in your IL instruction, did you determine your experience to be successful thanks to it seeming like it went well? Broken out by type of college.

Type of College	Yes	No
Community college	33.33%	66.67%
4-year college	10.00%	90.00%
MA-/PhD-granting college	9.09%	90.91%
Research university	27.27%	72.73%

Table 17.1.5 If you have used blended learning techniques in your IL instruction, did you determine your experience to be successful thanks to it seeming like it went well? Broken out by full-time equivalent enrollment of the college.

Enrollment	Yes	No
Less than 3,000	15.38%	84.62%
3,000 to 9,999	9.09%	90.91%
10,000 or more	29.41%	70.59%

Table 17.1.6 If you have used blended learning techniques in your IL instruction, did you determine your experience to be successful thanks to it seeming like it went well? Broken out by age of participant.

Age Range	Yes	No
Under 40	25.00%	75.00%
40 to 49	30.77%	69.23%
50 and over	6.25%	93.75%

If you used another method not listed above to determine the success of your blended learning IL instruction experience, please specify.

1. Feedback from the faculty member that students found this helpful and that projects were improved from the previous semester.

2. Course evaluations and post and pre test analysis of student learning outcomes.

3. There's an assumption.

4. Working on integrating formal assessment this year.

5. We used a SurveyMonkey for assessment.

6. Faculty gave it high marks. This was the first year for it.

7. Students in the flipped sessions scored about 20 points higher on the post-test administered at the semester's end.

8. Faculty feedback.

9. The instructor saw increased quality of sources and increased quantity of sources from library databases.

Table 18 If you have used blended learning techniques in your IL instruction, were they used in face-to-face instruction?[*]

Table 18.1.1 If you have used blended learning techniques in your IL instruction, were they used in face-to-face instruction?

	Yes	No
Entire sample	70.73%	29.27%

Table 18.1.2 If you have used blended learning techniques in your IL instruction, were they used in face-to-face instruction? Broken out by public or private status of the college.

Public or Private	Yes	No
Public	61.54%	38.46%
Private	86.67%	13.33%

Table 18.1.3 If you have used blended learning techniques in your IL instruction, were they used in face-to-face instruction? Broken out by annual full-time tuition prior to any deductions.

Tuition	Yes	No
Less than $5,000	69.23%	30.77%
$5,000 to $9,999	75.00%	25.00%
$10,000 to $24,999	57.14%	42.86%
$25,000 or more	90.00%	10.00%

Table 18.1.4 If you have used blended learning techniques in your IL instruction, were they used in face-to-face instruction? Broken out by type of college.

Type of College	Yes	No
Community college	77.78%	22.22%
4-year college	80.00%	20.00%
MA-/PhD-granting college	63.64%	36.36%
Research university	63.64%	36.36%

---

[*] Respondents to this question include only those participants who have used blended learning techniques in IL instruction, as per Table 13

Table 18.1.5 If you have used blended learning techniques in your IL instruction, were they used in face-to-face instruction? Broken out by full-time equivalent enrollment of the college.

Enrollment	Yes	No
Less than 3,000	84.62%	15.38%
3,000 to 9,999	81.82%	18.18%
10,000 or more	52.94%	47.06%

Table 18.1.6 If you have used blended learning techniques in your IL instruction, were they used in face-to-face instruction? Broken out by age of participant.

Age Range	Yes	No
Under 40	91.67%	8.33%
40 to 49	76.92%	23.08%
50 and over	50.00%	50.00%

Table 19 If you have used blended learning techniques in your IL instruction, were they used in online instruction?[*]

Table 19.1.1 If you have used blended learning techniques in your IL instruction, were they used in online instruction?

	Yes	No
Entire sample	29.27%	70.73%

Table 19.1.2 If you have used blended learning techniques in your IL instruction, were they used in online instruction? Broken out by public or private status of the college.

Public or Private	Yes	No
Public	30.77%	69.23%
Private	26.67%	73.33%

Table 19.1.3 If you have used blended learning techniques in your IL instruction, were they used in online instruction? Broken out by annual full-time tuition prior to any deductions.

Tuition	Yes	No
Less than $5,000	15.38%	84.62%
$5,000 to $9,999	25.00%	75.00%
$10,000 to $24,999	42.86%	57.14%
$25,000 or more	30.00%	70.00%

Table 19.1.4 If you have used blended learning techniques in your IL instruction, were they used in online instruction? Broken out by type of college.

Type of College	Yes	No
Community college	11.11%	88.89%
4-year college	40.00%	60.00%
MA-/PhD-granting college	18.18%	81.82%
Research university	45.45%	54.55%

[*] Respondents to this question include only those participants who have used blended learning techniques in IL instruction, as per Table 13

Table 19.1.5 If you have used blended learning techniques in your IL instruction, were they used in online instruction? Broken out by full-time equivalent enrollment of the college.

Enrollment	Yes	No
Less than 3,000	30.77%	69.23%
3,000 to 9,999	9.09%	90.91%
10,000 or more	41.18%	58.82%

Table 19.1.6 If you have used blended learning techniques in your IL instruction, were they used in online instruction? Broken out by age of participant.

Age Range	Yes	No
Under 40	8.33%	91.67%
40 to 49	30.77%	69.23%
50 and over	43.75%	56.25%

Table 20 If you have used blended learning techniques in your IL instruction, were they used in hybrid (face-to-face and online) instruction?*

Table 20.1.1 If you have used blended learning techniques in your IL instruction, were they used in hybrid (face-to-face and online) instruction?

	Yes	No
Entire sample	29.27%	70.73%

Table 20.1.2 If you have used blended learning techniques in your IL instruction, were they used in hybrid (face-to-face and online) instruction? Broken out by public or private status of the college.

Public or Private	Yes	No
Public	38.46%	61.54%
Private	13.33%	86.67%

Table 20.1.3 If you have used blended learning techniques in your IL instruction, were they used in hybrid (face-to-face and online) instruction? Broken out by annual full-time tuition prior to any deductions.

Tuition	Yes	No
Less than $5,000	46.15%	53.85%
$5,000 to $9,999	25.00%	75.00%
$10,000 to $24,999	28.57%	71.43%
$25,000 or more	10.00%	90.00%

Table 20.1.4 If you have used blended learning techniques in your IL instruction, were they used in hybrid (face-to-face and online) instruction? Broken out by type of college.

Type of College	Yes	No
Community college	44.44%	55.56%
4-year college	30.00%	70.00%
MA-/PhD-granting college	18.18%	81.82%
Research university	27.27%	72.73%

---

* Respondents to this question include only those participants who have used blended learning techniques in IL instruction, as per Table 13

Table 20.1.5 If you have used blended learning techniques in your IL instruction, were they used in hybrid (face-to-face and online) instruction? Broken out by full-time equivalent enrollment of the college.

Enrollment	Yes	No
Less than 3,000	15.38%	84.62%
3,000 to 9,999	36.36%	63.64%
10,000 or more	35.29%	64.71%

Table 20.1.6 If you have used blended learning techniques in your IL instruction, were they used in hybrid (face-to-face and online) instruction? Broken out by age of participant.

Age Range	Yes	No
Under 40	16.67%	83.33%
40 to 49	30.77%	69.23%
50 and over	37.50%	62.50%

Briefly describe a successful blended learning IL instruction experience you have had.

1. Piloted video tutorials to prep students for class (flipped model). Successful but need to build on the pilot. Worked well when faculty assigned the videos. Also very useful in responding to e-reference, especially text.

2. Prepared an exercise for students to do using our discovery system.

3. Assigning keyword brainstorming worksheets prior to a session. Minimal lecture in favor of group work and activities.

4. We teach a creadit bearing half semester IL course online with one or two face-to-face meetings.

5. Before a scheduled IL session students were assigned and quizzed on a study guide I created. The IL sessions began with a discussion of research concepts - students led the discussion, asked additional questions.

6. Our freshman ENG comp classes have an online module that students complete on their own with worksheets, prior to a workshop experience with their faculty and librarians.

7. It really depends on the class. Success is generally determined by how engaged the students are, how much/little technology savvy they possess, and whether they are in developmental or general education courses.

8. Using webinar for synchronous ans asynchronous learning.

9. Embedded librarian in online class.

10. Offering tutorials, remote online research sessions, online supplementary materials and use of online materials in the classroom.

11. Watch online video prior to coming to library.

12. We developed a short tutorial that student's take before coming to their required second semester freshman year that teaches the mechanics of database searching. In this session we also use an online game I developed about evaluating information.

13. I had students view two general tutorials (using our online catalog & Finding Articles) so that I could follow up on skills there and focus on what their questions were on access/mechanics so that the focus of the session could be on evaluating the sources the students find in those places.

14. Use of screencasts for students to work through independently then classroom assignments to consolidate learning.

15. Students engaged with interactive tutorial prior to inclass session.

16. Not much success. Students did not do the reading or exercises.

17. Use of online tutorial before face to face instruction.

18. Created online tutorial for using discovery tool.

19. Using voice over with PowerPoint and Prezi.

20. Working with international students, embedded in their writing class, teaching 8 week course on basic library use and research.

21. Face-to-face instruction and online assessed exercises.

22. I was embedded in an English course and was able to infused information literacy throughout the semester.

23. Brief 15 minute visit to the classroom and gave a pre-test/survey for a specific graduate summer class, a few years in a row. Also created a Prezi for the class one year.

24. In a collaborative session w/ first year Required English writing course, the whys and hows of citation are now done as a required online module combined with an online assessment.

25. Despite the aids provided in advance, f2f was necessary.

26. Mostly using our LMS to post surveys/quizzes before class - these sometimes include video and sometimes just text.

27. Students view several videos and complete quizzes before the class session. (First-Year Experience course).

28. Brief instruction/demonstration alternated with hands on activity with smartphones/tablets. Or, assigning reading and tutorials beforehand, with hands-on, guided practice in the instruction session.

29. We used an online survey to assess student ability, they then attended a face to face workshop which included the use of online chat and then they fed back to the instructor via a VLE.

30. Our ULIB 101 -- Introduction to Library Research class (1 credit) is flipped.

This is the second year. I collaborated with an English faculty member this spring to flip the IL instruction for the class.

31. I'm embedded in an ENG 102 advanced composition class in a computer lab. It worked very well are class filled up much faster than other ENG 102 classes that are offered on campus.

32. Have students read a research article and a PowerPoint, then complete a worksheet, at home before library session. Soon we will start to use more online videos and tutorials.

33. We did a video workshop but instead of providing the editing instruction in the class, I made a video for them about basic editing using the tool for that project (iMovie) - they watched ahead of time so that during the class, they could work in groups on the actual project with the opportunity to talk through storyboard issues with their English instructor and editing issues with me.

34. Students were required to create the library tutorial. Each group was given a section and had to demonstrate it for the class.

35. I created the media pieces and helped design this website that we have used to flip instruction: http://esulibinstruction.weebly.com/

Table 21 If you have used blended learning techniques in your IL instruction, did you use videos created by you (or the library) in your instruction?*

Table 21.1.1 If you have used blended learning techniques in your IL instruction, did you use videos created by you (or the library) in your instruction?

	Yes	No
Entire sample	46.34%	53.66%

Table 21.1.2 If you have used blended learning techniques in your IL instruction, did you use videos created by you (or the library) in your instruction? Broken out by public or private status of the college.

Public or Private	Yes	No
Public	53.85%	46.15%
Private	33.33%	66.67%

Table 21.1.3 If you have used blended learning techniques in your IL instruction, did you use videos created by you (or the library) in your instruction? Broken out by annual full-time tuition prior to any deductions.

Tuition	Yes	No
Less than $5,000	53.85%	46.15%
$5,000 to $9,999	50.00%	50.00%
$10,000 to $24,999	50.00%	50.00%
$25,000 or more	30.00%	70.00%

Table 21.1.4 If you have used blended learning techniques in your IL instruction, did you use videos created by you (or the library) in your instruction? Broken out by type of college.

Type of College	Yes	No
Community college	55.56%	44.44%
4-year college	20.00%	80.00%
MA-/PhD-granting college	45.45%	54.55%
Research university	63.64%	36.36%

* Respondents to this question include only those participants who have used blended learning techniques in IL instruction, as per Table 13

108

Table 21.1.5 If you have used blended learning techniques in your IL instruction, did you use videos created by you (or the library) in your instruction? Broken out by full-time equivalent enrollment of the college.

Enrollment	Yes	No
Less than 3,000	38.46%	61.54%
3,000 to 9,999	27.27%	72.73%
10,000 or more	64.71%	35.29%

Table 21.1.6 If you have used blended learning techniques in your IL instruction, did you use videos created by you (or the library) in your instruction? Broken out by age of participant.

Age Range	Yes	No
Under 40	25.00%	75.00%
40 to 49	53.85%	46.15%
50 and over	56.25%	43.75%

Table 22 If you have used blended learning techniques in your IL instruction, did you use readings created by you (or the library) in your instruction?[*]

Table 22.1.1 If you have used blended learning techniques in your IL instruction, did you use readings created by you (or the library) in your instruction?

	Yes	No
Entire sample	24.39%	75.61%

Table 22.1.2 If you have used blended learning techniques in your IL instruction, did you use readings created by you (or the library) in your instruction? Broken out by public or private status of the college.

Public or Private	Yes	No
Public	23.08%	76.92%
Private	26.67%	73.33%

Table 22.1.3 If you have used blended learning techniques in your IL instruction, did you use readings created by you (or the library) in your instruction? Broken out by annual full-time tuition prior to any deductions.

Tuition	Yes	No
Less than $5,000	15.38%	84.62%
$5,000 to $9,999	50.00%	50.00%
$10,000 to $24,999	28.57%	71.43%
$25,000 or more	20.00%	80.00%

Table 22.1.4 If you have used blended learning techniques in your IL instruction, did you use readings created by you (or the library) in your instruction? Broken out by type of college.

Type of College	Yes	No
Community college	11.11%	88.89%
4-year college	10.00%	90.00%
MA-/PhD-granting college	36.36%	63.64%
Research university	36.36%	63.64%

[*] Respondents to this question include only those participants who have used blended learning techniques in IL instruction, as per Table 13

Table 22.1.5 If you have used blended learning techniques in your IL instruction, did you use readings created by you (or the library) in your instruction? Broken out by full-time equivalent enrollment of the college.

Enrollment	Yes	No
Less than 3,000	15.38%	84.62%
3,000 to 9,999	27.27%	72.73%
10,000 or more	29.41%	70.59%

Table 22.1.6 If you have used blended learning techniques in your IL instruction, did you use readings created by you (or the library) in your instruction? Broken out by age of participant.

Age Range	Yes	No
Under 40	16.67%	83.33%
40 to 49	23.08%	76.92%
50 and over	31.25%	68.75%

Table 23 If you have used blended learning techniques in your IL instruction, did you use discussion questions created by you (or the library) in your instruction?[*]

Table 23.1.1 If you have used blended learning techniques in your IL instruction, did you use discussion questions created by you (or the library) in your instruction?

	Yes	No
Entire sample	48.78%	51.22%

Table 23.1.2 If you have used blended learning techniques in your IL instruction, did you use discussion questions created by you (or the library) in your instruction? Broken out by public or private status of the college.

Public or Private	Yes	No
Public	53.85%	46.15%
Private	40.00%	60.00%

Table 23.1.3 If you have used blended learning techniques in your IL instruction, did you use discussion questions created by you (or the library) in your instruction? Broken out by annual full-time tuition prior to any deductions.

Tuition	Yes	No
Less than $5,000	53.85%	46.15%
$5,000 to $9,999	50.00%	50.00%
$10,000 to $24,999	57.14%	42.86%
$25,000 or more	30.00%	70.00%

---

[*] Respondents to this question include only those participants who have used blended learning techniques in IL instruction, as per Table 13

Table 23.1.4 If you have used blended learning techniques in your IL instruction, did you use discussion questions created by you (or the library) in your instruction? Broken out by type of college.

Type of College	Yes	No
Community college	55.56%	44.44%
4-year college	30.00%	70.00%
MA-/PhD-granting college	54.55%	45.45%
Research university	54.55%	45.45%

Table 23.1.5 If you have used blended learning techniques in your IL instruction, did you use discussion questions created by you (or the library) in your instruction? Broken out by full-time equivalent enrollment of the college.

Enrollment	Yes	No
Less than 3,000	46.15%	53.85%
3,000 to 9,999	36.36%	63.64%
10,000 or more	58.82%	41.18%

Table 23.1.6 If you have used blended learning techniques in your IL instruction, did you use discussion questions created by you (or the library) in your instruction? Broken out by age of participant.

Age Range	Yes	No
Under 40	25.00%	75.00%
40 to 49	38.46%	61.54%
50 and over	75.00%	25.00%

Table 24 If you have used blended learning techniques in your IL instruction, did you use pre-tests created by you (or the library) in your instruction?*

Table 24.1.1 If you have used blended learning techniques in your IL instruction, did you use pre-tests created by you (or the library) in your instruction?

	Yes	No
Entire sample	24.39%	75.61%

Table 24.1.2 If you have used blended learning techniques in your IL instruction, did you use pre-tests created by you (or the library) in your instruction? Broken out by public or private status of the college.

Public or Private	Yes	No
Public	23.08%	76.92%
Private	26.67%	73.33%

Table 24.1.3 If you have used blended learning techniques in your IL instruction, did you use pre-tests created by you (or the library) in your instruction? Broken out by annual full-time tuition prior to any deductions.

Tuition	Yes	No
Less than $5,000	30.77%	69.23%
$5,000 to $9,999	50.00%	50.00%
$10,000 to $24,999	7.14%	92.86%
$25,000 or more	30.00%	70.00%

Table 24.1.4 If you have used blended learning techniques in your IL instruction, did you use pre-tests created by you (or the library) in your instruction? Broken out by type of college.

Type of College	Yes	No
Community college	33.33%	66.67%
4-year college	10.00%	90.00%
MA-/PhD-granting college	27.27%	72.73%
Research university	27.27%	72.73%

---

* Respondents to this question include only those participants who have used blended learning techniques in IL instruction, as per Table 13

Table 24.1.5 If you have used blended learning techniques in your IL instruction, did you use pre-tests created by you (or the library) in your instruction? Broken out by full-time equivalent enrollment of the college.

Enrollment	Yes	No
Less than 3,000	15.38%	84.62%
3,000 to 9,999	27.27%	72.73%
10,000 or more	29.41%	70.59%

Table 24.1.6 If you have used blended learning techniques in your IL instruction, did you use pre-tests created by you (or the library) in your instruction? Broken out by age of participant.

Age Range	Yes	No
Under 40	8.33%	91.67%
40 to 49	23.08%	76.92%
50 and over	37.50%	62.50%

Table 25 If you have used blended learning techniques in your IL instruction, did you use surveys created by you (or the library) in your instruction?[*]

Table 25.1.1 If you have used blended learning techniques in your IL instruction, did you use surveys created by you (or the library) in your instruction?

	Yes	No
Entire sample	43.90%	56.10%

Table 25.1.2 If you have used blended learning techniques in your IL instruction, did you use surveys created by you (or the library) in your instruction? Broken out by public or private status of the college.

Public or Private	Yes	No
Public	50.00%	50.00%
Private	33.33%	66.67%

Table 25.1.3 If you have used blended learning techniques in your IL instruction, did you use surveys created by you (or the library) in your instruction? Broken out by annual full-time tuition prior to any deductions.

Tuition	Yes	No
Less than $5,000	61.54%	38.46%
$5,000 to $9,999	50.00%	50.00%
$10,000 to $24,999	42.86%	57.14%
$25,000 or more	20.00%	80.00%

Table 25.1.4 If you have used blended learning techniques in your IL instruction, did you use surveys created by you (or the library) in your instruction? Broken out by type of college.

Type of College	Yes	No
Community college	77.78%	22.22%
4-year college	20.00%	80.00%
MA-/PhD-granting college	36.36%	63.64%
Research university	45.45%	54.55%

[*] Respondents to this question include only those participants who have used blended learning techniques in IL instruction, as per Table 13

Table 25.1.5 If you have used blended learning techniques in your IL instruction, did you use surveys created by you (or the library) in your instruction? Broken out by full-time equivalent enrollment of the college.

Enrollment	Yes	No
Less than 3,000	38.46%	61.54%
3,000 to 9,999	45.45%	54.55%
10,000 or more	47.06%	52.94%

Table 25.1.6 If you have used blended learning techniques in your IL instruction, did you use surveys created by you (or the library) in your instruction? Broken out by age of participant.

Age Range	Yes	No
Under 40	41.67%	58.33%
40 to 49	46.15%	53.85%
50 and over	43.75%	56.25%

Table 26 If you have used blended learning techniques in your IL instruction, did you use online tutorials created by you (or the library) in your instruction?[*]

Table 26.1.1 If you have used blended learning techniques in your IL instruction, did you use online tutorials created by you (or the library) in your instruction?

	Yes	No
Entire sample	46.34%	53.66%

Table 26.1.2 If you have used blended learning techniques in your IL instruction, did you use online tutorials created by you (or the library) in your instruction? Broken out by public or private status of the college.

Public or Private	Yes	No
Public	50.00%	50.00%
Private	40.00%	60.00%

Table 26.1.3 If you have used blended learning techniques in your IL instruction, did you use online tutorials created by you (or the library) in your instruction? Broken out by annual full-time tuition prior to any deductions.

Tuition	Yes	No
Less than $5,000	46.15%	53.85%
$5,000 to $9,999	50.00%	50.00%
$10,000 to $24,999	50.00%	50.00%
$25,000 or more	40.00%	60.00%

Table 26.1.4 If you have used blended learning techniques in your IL instruction, did you use online tutorials created by you (or the library) in your instruction? Broken out by type of college.

Type of College	Yes	No
Community college	33.33%	66.67%
4-year college	60.00%	40.00%
MA-/PhD-granting college	36.36%	63.64%
Research university	54.55%	45.45%

[*] Respondents to this question include only those participants who have used blended learning techniques in IL instruction, as per Table 13

Table 26.1.5 If you have used blended learning techniques in your IL instruction, did you use online tutorials created by you (or the library) in your instruction? Broken out by full-time equivalent enrollment of the college.

Enrollment	Yes	No
Less than 3,000	46.15%	53.85%
3,000 to 9,999	45.45%	54.55%
10,000 or more	47.06%	52.94%

Table 26.1.6 If you have used blended learning techniques in your IL instruction, did you use online tutorials created by you (or the library) in your instruction? Broken out by age of participant.

Age Range	Yes	No
Under 40	33.33%	66.67%
40 to 49	46.15%	53.85%
50 and over	56.25%	43.75%

Table 27 If you have used blended learning techniques in your IL instruction, did you use videos created by someone else (other than you or the library) in your instruction?[*]

Table 27.1.1 If you have used blended learning techniques in your IL instruction, did you use videos created by someone else (other than you or the library) in your instruction?

	Yes	No
Entire sample	26.83%	73.17%

Table 27.1.2 If you have used blended learning techniques in your IL instruction, did you use videos created by someone else (other than you or the library) in your instruction? Broken out by public or private status of the college.

Public or Private	Yes	No
Public	19.23%	80.77%
Private	40.00%	60.00%

Table 27.1.3 If you have used blended learning techniques in your IL instruction, did you use videos created by someone else (other than you or the library) in your instruction? Broken out by annual full-time tuition prior to any deductions.

Tuition	Yes	No
Less than $5,000	15.38%	84.62%
$5,000 to $9,999	25.00%	75.00%
$10,000 to $24,999	28.57%	71.43%
$25,000 or more	40.00%	60.00%

---

[*] Respondents to this question include only those participants who have used blended learning techniques in IL instruction, as per Table 13

Table 27.1.4 If you have used blended learning techniques in your IL instruction, did you use videos created by someone else (other than you or the library) in your instruction? Broken out by type of college.

Type of College	Yes	No
Community college	22.22%	77.78%
4-year college	30.00%	70.00%
MA-/PhD-granting college	27.27%	72.73%
Research university	27.27%	72.73%

Table 27.1.5 If you have used blended learning techniques in your IL instruction, did you use videos created by someone else (other than you or the library) in your instruction? Broken out by full-time equivalent enrollment of the college.

Enrollment	Yes	No
Less than 3,000	38.46%	61.54%
3,000 to 9,999	27.27%	72.73%
10,000 or more	17.65%	82.35%

Table 27.1.6 If you have used blended learning techniques in your IL instruction, did you use videos created by someone else (other than you or the library) in your instruction? Broken out by age of participant.

Age Range	Yes	No
Under 40	25.00%	75.00%
40 to 49	15.38%	84.62%
50 and over	37.50%	62.50%

Table 28 If you have used blended learning techniques in your IL instruction, did you use readings created by someone else (other than you or the library) in your instruction?[*]

Table 28.1.1 If you have used blended learning techniques in your IL instruction, did you use readings created by someone else (other than you or the library) in your instruction?

	Yes	No
Entire sample	21.95%	78.05%

Table 28.1.2 If you have used blended learning techniques in your IL instruction, did you use readings created by someone else (other than you or the library) in your instruction? Broken out by public or private status of the college.

Public or Private	Yes	No
Public	23.08%	76.92%
Private	20.00%	80.00%

Table 28.1.3 If you have used blended learning techniques in your IL instruction, did you use readings created by someone else (other than you or the library) in your instruction? Broken out by annual full-time tuition prior to any deductions.

Tuition	Yes	No
Less than $5,000	30.77%	69.23%
$5,000 to $9,999	0.00%	100.00%
$10,000 to $24,999	21.43%	78.57%
$25,000 or more	20.00%	80.00%

---

[*] Respondents to this question include only those participants who have used blended learning techniques in IL instruction, as per Table 13

Table 28.1.4 If you have used blended learning techniques in your IL instruction, did you use readings created by someone else (other than you or the library) in your instruction? Broken out by type of college.

Type of College	Yes	No
Community college	44.44%	55.56%
4-year college	30.00%	70.00%
MA-/PhD-granting college	0.00%	100.00%
Research university	18.18%	81.82%

Table 28.1.5 If you have used blended learning techniques in your IL instruction, did you use readings created by someone else (other than you or the library) in your instruction? Broken out by full-time equivalent enrollment of the college.

Enrollment	Yes	No
Less than 3,000	30.77%	69.23%
3,000 to 9,999	9.09%	90.91%
10,000 or more	23.53%	76.47%

Table 28.1.6 If you have used blended learning techniques in your IL instruction, did you use readings created by someone else (other than you or the library) in your instruction? Broken out by age of participant.

Age Range	Yes	No
Under 40	16.67%	83.33%
40 to 49	23.08%	76.92%
50 and over	25.00%	75.00%

Table 29 If you have used blended learning techniques in your IL instruction, did you use discussion questions created by someone else (other than you or the library) in your instruction?[*]

Table 29.1.1 If you have used blended learning techniques in your IL instruction, did you use discussion questions created by someone else (other than you or the library) in your instruction?

	Yes	No
Entire sample	9.76%	90.24%

Table 29.1.2 If you have used blended learning techniques in your IL instruction, did you use discussion questions created by someone else (other than you or the library) in your instruction? Broken out by public or private status of the college.

Public or Private	Yes	No
Public	7.69%	92.31%
Private	13.33%	86.67%

Table 29.1.3 If you have used blended learning techniques in your IL instruction, did you use discussion questions created by someone else (other than you or the library) in your instruction? Broken out by annual full-time tuition prior to any deductions.

Tuition	Yes	No
Less than $5,000	15.38%	84.62%
$5,000 to $9,999	0.00%	100.00%
$10,000 to $24,999	7.14%	92.86%
$25,000 or more	10.00%	90.00%

---

[*] Respondents to this question include only those participants who have used blended learning techniques in IL instruction, as per Table 13

Table 29.1.4 If you have used blended learning techniques in your IL instruction, did you use discussion questions created by someone else (other than you or the library) in your instruction? Broken out by type of college.

Type of College	Yes	No
Community college	22.22%	77.78%
4-year college	10.00%	90.00%
MA-/PhD-granting college	9.09%	90.91%
Research university	0.00%	100.00%

Table 29.1.5 If you have used blended learning techniques in your IL instruction, did you use discussion questions created by someone else (other than you or the library) in your instruction? Broken out by full-time equivalent enrollment of the college.

Enrollment	Yes	No
Less than 3,000	23.08%	76.92%
3,000 to 9,999	0.00%	100.00%
10,000 or more	5.88%	94.12%

Table 29.1.6 If you have used blended learning techniques in your IL instruction, did you use discussion questions created by someone else (other than you or the library) in your instruction? Broken out by age of participant.

Age Range	Yes	No
Under 40	25.00%	75.00%
40 to 49	7.69%	92.31%
50 and over	0.00%	100.00%

Table 30 If you have used blended learning techniques in your IL instruction, did you use pre-tests created by someone else (other than you or the library) in your instruction?[*]

Table 30.1.1 If you have used blended learning techniques in your IL instruction, did you use pre-tests created by someone else (other than you or the library) in your instruction?

	Yes	No
Entire sample	7.32%	92.68%

Table 30.1.2 If you have used blended learning techniques in your IL instruction, did you use pre-tests created by someone else (other than you or the library) in your instruction? Broken out by public or private status of the college.

Public or Private	Yes	No
Public	7.69%	92.31%
Private	6.67%	93.33%

Table 30.1.3 If you have used blended learning techniques in your IL instruction, did you use pre-tests created by someone else (other than you or the library) in your instruction? Broken out by annual full-time tuition prior to any deductions.

Tuition	Yes	No
Less than $5,000	15.38%	84.62%
$5,000 to $9,999	0.00%	100.00%
$10,000 to $24,999	0.00%	100.00%
$25,000 or more	10.00%	90.00%

---

[*] Respondents to this question include only those participants who have used blended learning techniques in IL instruction, as per Table 13

Table 30.1.4 If you have used blended learning techniques in your IL instruction, did you use pre-tests created by someone else (other than you or the library) in your instruction? Broken out by type of college.

Type of College	Yes	No
Community college	22.22%	77.78%
4-year college	10.00%	90.00%
MA-/PhD-granting college	0.00%	100.00%
Research university	0.00%	100.00%

Table 30.1.5 If you have used blended learning techniques in your IL instruction, did you use pre-tests created by someone else (other than you or the library) in your instruction? Broken out by full-time equivalent enrollment of the college.

Enrollment	Yes	No
Less than 3,000	15.38%	84.62%
3,000 to 9,999	0.00%	100.00%
10,000 or more	5.88%	94.12%

Table 30.1.6 If you have used blended learning techniques in your IL instruction, did you use pre-tests created by someone else (other than you or the library) in your instruction? Broken out by age of participant.

Age Range	Yes	No
Under 40	8.33%	91.67%
40 to 49	7.69%	92.31%
50 and over	6.25%	93.75%

Table 31 If you have used blended learning techniques in your IL instruction, did you use surveys created by someone else (other than you or the library) in your instruction?[*]

Table 31.1.1 If you have used blended learning techniques in your IL instruction, did you use surveys created by someone else (other than you or the library) in your instruction?

	Yes	No
Entire sample	9.76%	90.24%

Table 31.1.2 If you have used blended learning techniques in your IL instruction, did you use surveys created by someone else (other than you or the library) in your instruction? Broken out by public or private status of the college.

Public or Private	Yes	No
Public	7.69%	92.31%
Private	13.33%	86.67%

Table 31.1.3 If you have used blended learning techniques in your IL instruction, did you use surveys created by someone else (other than you or the library) in your instruction? Broken out by annual full-time tuition prior to any deductions.

Tuition	Yes	No
Less than $5,000	15.38%	84.62%
$5,000 to $9,999	0.00%	100.00%
$10,000 to $24,999	0.00%	100.00%
$25,000 or more	20.00%	80.00%

---

[*] Respondents to this question include only those participants who have used blended learning techniques in IL instruction, as per Table 13

Table 31.1.4 If you have used blended learning techniques in your IL instruction, did you use surveys created by someone else (other than you or the library) in your instruction? Broken out by type of college.

Type of College	Yes	No
Community college	22.22%	77.78%
4-year college	10.00%	90.00%
MA-/PhD-granting college	9.09%	90.91%
Research university	0.00%	100.00%

Table 31.1.5 If you have used blended learning techniques in your IL instruction, did you use surveys created by someone else (other than you or the library) in your instruction? Broken out by full-time equivalent enrollment of the college.

Enrollment	Yes	No
Less than 3,000	15.38%	84.62%
3,000 to 9,999	0.00%	100.00%
10,000 or more	11.76%	88.24%

Table 31.1.6 If you have used blended learning techniques in your IL instruction, did you use surveys created by someone else (other than you or the library) in your instruction? Broken out by age of participant.

Age Range	Yes	No
Under 40	16.67%	83.33%
40 to 49	15.38%	84.62%
50 and over	0.00%	100.00%

Table 32 If you have used blended learning techniques in your IL instruction, did you use online tutorials created by someone else (other than you or the library) in your instruction?[*]

Table 32.1.1 If you have used blended learning techniques in your IL instruction, did you use online tutorials created by someone else (other than you or the library) in your instruction?

	Yes	No
Entire sample	17.07%	82.93%

Table 32.1.2 If you have used blended learning techniques in your IL instruction, did you use online tutorials created by someone else (other than you or the library) in your instruction? Broken out by public or private status of the college.

Public or Private	Yes	No
Public	7.69%	92.31%
Private	33.33%	66.67%

Table 32.1.3 If you have used blended learning techniques in your IL instruction, did you use online tutorials created by someone else (other than you or the library) in your instruction? Broken out by annual full-time tuition prior to any deductions.

Tuition	Yes	No
Less than $5,000	7.69%	92.31%
$5,000 to $9,999	25.00%	75.00%
$10,000 to $24,999	21.43%	78.57%
$25,000 or more	20.00%	80.00%

[*] Respondents to this question include only those participants who have used blended learning techniques in IL instruction, as per Table 13

Table 32.1.4 If you have used blended learning techniques in your IL instruction, did you use online tutorials created by someone else (other than you or the library) in your instruction? Broken out by type of college.

Type of College	Yes	No
Community college	11.11%	88.89%
4-year college	30.00%	70.00%
MA-/PhD-granting college	18.18%	81.82%
Research university	9.09%	90.91%

Table 32.1.5 If you have used blended learning techniques in your IL instruction, did you use online tutorials created by someone else (other than you or the library) in your instruction? Broken out by full-time equivalent enrollment of the college.

Enrollment	Yes	No
Less than 3,000	30.77%	69.23%
3,000 to 9,999	18.18%	81.82%
10,000 or more	5.88%	94.12%

Table 32.1.6 If you have used blended learning techniques in your IL instruction, did you use online tutorials created by someone else (other than you or the library) in your instruction? Broken out by age of participant.

Age Range	Yes	No
Under 40	25.00%	75.00%
40 to 49	15.38%	84.62%
50 and over	12.50%	87.50%

If you have used blended learning techniques in your IL instruction and have used in your instruction any other assignments or supplemental materials not listed above, please specify.

1. We collaborated on classroom activities and exercises taking turns and breaking classroom instruction into chunks.

2. I created a handout for each group.

3. Google Calendar with video playlist, Google Sites with links to all calendars, videos, assignment calculator schedule, and research log.

4. Online graded quiz with results to instructor and librarians.

5. Quizzes on the material.

6. Instructional podcasts created by our staff.

7. I also created the worksheets we used in the instruction.

8. Exercises.

9. Online game - created by me.

10. Worksheet.

Table 33 If you have used blended learning techniques in your IL instruction, approximately how long did it take to prepare this instruction session?[*]

Table 33.1.1 If you have used blended learning techniques in your IL instruction, approximately how long did it take to prepare this instruction session?

	Less than 1 day	1-7 days	More than 1 week	Don't know
Entire sample	17.07%	31.71%	39.02%	12.20%

Table 33.1.2 If you have used blended learning techniques in your IL instruction, approximately how long did it take to prepare this instruction session? Broken out by public or private status of the college.

Public or Private	Less than 1 day	1-7 days	More than 1 week	Don't know
Public	15.38%	23.08%	46.15%	15.38%
Private	20.00%	46.67%	26.67%	6.67%

Table 33.1.3 If you have used blended learning techniques in your IL instruction, approximately how long did it take to prepare this instruction session? Broken out by annual full-time tuition prior to any deductions.

Tuition	Less than 1 day	1-7 days	More than 1 week	Don't know
Less than $5,000	7.69%	23.08%	61.54%	7.69%
$5,000 to $9,999	50.00%	0.00%	25.00%	25.00%
$10,000 to $24,999	14.29%	42.86%	28.57%	14.29%
$25,000 or more	20.00%	40.00%	30.00%	10.00%

---

[*] Respondents to this question include only those participants who have used blended learning techniques in IL instruction, as per Table 13

Table 33.1.4 If you have used blended learning techniques in your IL instruction, approximately how long did it take to prepare this instruction session? Broken out by type of college.

Type of College	Less than 1 day	1-7 days	More than 1 week	Don't know
Community college	0.00%	44.44%	44.44%	11.11%
4-year college	30.00%	20.00%	50.00%	0.00%
MA-/PhD-granting college	9.09%	54.55%	18.18%	18.18%
Research university	27.27%	9.09%	45.45%	18.18%

Table 33.1.5 If you have used blended learning techniques in your IL instruction, approximately how long did it take to prepare this instruction session? Broken out by full-time equivalent enrollment of the college.

Enrollment	Less than 1 day	1-7 days	More than 1 week	Don't know
Less than 3,000	23.08%	46.15%	23.08%	7.69%
3,000 to 9,999	9.09%	18.18%	63.64%	9.09%
10,000 or more	17.65%	29.41%	35.29%	17.65%

Table 33.1.6 If you have used blended learning techniques in your IL instruction, approximately how long did it take to prepare this instruction session? Broken out by age of participant.

Age Range	Less than 1 day	1-7 days	More than 1 week	Don't know
Under 40	16.67%	66.67%	16.67%	0.00%
40 to 49	15.38%	23.08%	46.15%	15.38%
50 and over	18.75%	12.50%	50.00%	18.75%

What advice would you give to other librarians interested in using blended learning techniques?

1. Needs time to do it right - should only use it if there are sound pedagogical reasons to do so.

2. If you are working with a faculty member in their class, plan the activity you wish to do during the class time so that it can inform the materials you create and give to the students ahead of time - it makes more planning work on the front end but the class is much more productive.

3. Work with the instruction of the class to create very specific outcomes. Don't be too worried if they don't do everything perfectly.

4. Be prepared to keep the students active. I try to spend more time having the students searching and actively evaluating so that they find the time valuable and they are engaged and seeing the value of our instruction time.

5. Make sure you have faculty support if you plan to ask for activities to be done outside of normal class time.

6. Know the difference between blending and flipping. BlendKit is a great course to check out.

7. I think ours is too wordy, but we are streamlining this summer. Keep texts more simple. Also, there are so many good components online to be found.

8. It often takes a lot of in-class scaffolding and structure to make the lesson resonate.

9. It is time consuming but worth it to create a lesson that engages students effectively, supports IL outcomes, course learning outcomes, and university learning outcomes.

10. Experiment, test, experience.

11. Keep trying!

12. Try a bit, start small. Keep the overall IL teaching practices at the forefront. ("As a result of interacting with the e-learning/hybrid module, students will be able to _____ in order to _____.")

13. Have not had experience in this area.

14. Need full support of IT department to add software.

15. It takes much more time than I anticipated. Students will have many questions (a good thing).

16. Be open-minded, be willing to fail. You will learn a lot more from things that go badly than things that go well.

17. It works very well. We were able to collaborate pretty well. It takes a little while to get accustomed to team teaching.

18. Read and be familiar with the successful progress of others in the profession.

19. If your students don't have this ability, they are unprepared and they feel 'they' have failed. We fail if we do not do this at any age K-18.

20. Make sure you have a recent computer with a lot of processing power and the right software. Start off with free resources and as you become more expert, move up to paid/more sophisticated programs. Try to attend workshops or locate tutorials to help you with your design and use of the software. Be brave! Don't fear failure -- just keep editing until it is what you want.

21. It is worth the effort!

22. Re-use materials - don't reinvent the wheel. Go for it! Don't be afraid to experiment.

23. Flipping is a fantastic technique. Providing a good portion of the instruction ahead of time allowed me to touch on some other concepts that might not otherwise receive attention in instruction--the majority of our instruction comes during comp sessions (2-3 depending on the class).

24. Learn how to do it!

25. Have to have instructor cooperation.

26. Breakdown content into smaller chunks than you think necessary.

27. Experiment! Also, we decided to make videos that were quick and easy and so not perfect at all. We liked this approach-- if we have to redo them in the future (as is often the case as things change) it isn't too much of a burden.

28. Practice it with a small group first. It is harder than it looks and others (including faculty members) overestimate what they can do and how fast they can do it. Don't over schedule.

29. Start small, pay attention to design considerations up front, focus on concepts, consider accessibility.

30. Sometimes the best time to try a blended learning technique is when you're already preparing for an instruction session that happens to lend itself well to it for one reason or another - often the variable is working with a professor who is supportive of library instruction and open to trying something new.

31. Plan each step carefully, attempt to build assessment into the learning process.

32. Preparation time is so important, practice with colleagues if you can before running the session and a "back up" plan if the technology fails.

33. Be careful what you wish for---have to be very attentive to online students who are requesting help at all hours of the day and night!

Chapter 3 – Classroom Response Systems

Table 34 Does your library currently use classroom response systems (popularly known as "clickers") in any of your information literacy classes?

Table 34.1.1 Does your library currently use classroom response systems (popularly known as "clickers") in any of your information literacy classes?

	No Answer	Yes	No
Entire sample	38.10%	23.81%	38.10%

Table 34.1.2 Does your library currently use classroom response systems (popularly known as "clickers") in any of your information literacy classes? Broken out by public or private status of the college.

Public or Private	No Answer	Yes	No
Public	36.84%	31.58%	31.58%
Private	40.00%	12.00%	48.00%

Table 34.1.3 Does your library currently use classroom response systems (popularly known as "clickers") in any of your information literacy classes? Broken out by annual full-time tuition prior to any deductions.

Tuition	No Answer	Yes	No
Less than $5,000	27.78%	11.11%	61.11%
$5,000 to $9,999	60.00%	30.00%	10.00%
$10,000 to $24,999	29.41%	47.06%	23.53%
$25,000 or more	44.44%	11.11%	44.44%

Table 34.1.4 Does your library currently use classroom response systems (popularly known as "clickers") in any of your information literacy classes? Broken out by type of college.

Type of College	No Answer	Yes	No
Community college	47.06%	5.88%	47.06%
Research university	28.57%	7.14%	64.29%
MA-/PhD-granting college	33.33%	26.67%	40.00%
Research university	41.18%	52.94%	5.88%

Table 34.1.5 Does your library currently use classroom response systems (popularly known as "clickers") in any of your information literacy classes? Broken out by full-time equivalent enrollment of the college.

Enrollment	No Answer	Yes	No
Less than 3,000	31.58%	15.79%	52.63%
10,000 or more	47.62%	4.76%	47.62%
10,000 or more	34.78%	47.83%	17.39%

Table 34.1.6 Does your library currently use classroom response systems (popularly known as "clickers") in any of your information literacy classes? Broken out by age of participant.

Age Range	No Answer	Yes	No
Under 40	47.83%	17.39%	34.78%
40 to 49	27.78%	38.89%	33.33%
50 and over	36.36%	18.18%	45.45%

If so, which brands do you use?

1. Turning Point.

2. Turning Point.

3. Turning point.

4. Own university developed.

5. Storify.

6. iClicker.

7. Optivote.

8. I can't remember.

9. TurningPoint.

10. iClicker.

11. i-clicker.

12. Turning point.

13. iclicker.

14. Near Pod.

Table 35 What are your library's plans for classroom response systems?

Table 35.1.1 What are your library's plans for classroom response systems?

	No Answer	Do not currently use nor do we plan to	Do not currently suse but plan to introduce	Currently use but plan to use it less	Currently use and have no plans to change usage level	Currently use and plan to use it more
Entire sample	39.68%	28.57%	9.52%	6.35%	11.11%	4.76%

Table 35.1.2 What are your library's plans for classroom response systems? Broken out by public or private status of the college.

Public or Private	No Answer	Do not currently use nor do we plan to	Do not currently suse but plan to introduce	Currently use but plan to use it less	Currently use and have no plans to change usage level	Currently use and plan to use it more
Public	39.47%	18.42%	10.53%	10.53%	15.79%	5.26%
Private	40.00%	44.00%	8.00%	0.00%	4.00%	4.00%

Table 35.1.3 What are your library's plans for classroom response systems? Broken out by annual full-time tuition prior to any deductions.

Tuition	No Answer	Do not currently use nor do we plan to	Do not currently suse but plan to introduce	Currently use but plan to use it less	Currently use and have no plans to change usage level	Currently use and plan to use it more
Less than $5,000	33.33%	33.33%	22.22%	0.00%	5.56%	5.56%
$5,000 to $9,999	60.00%	10.00%	0.00%	0.00%	20.00%	10.00%
$10,000 to $24,999	29.41%	23.53%	0.00%	23.53%	23.53%	0.00%
$25,000 or more	44.44%	38.89%	11.11%	0.00%	0.00%	5.56%

Table 35.1.4 What are your library's plans for classroom response systems? Broken out by type of college.

Type of College	No Answer	Do not currently use nor do we plan to	Do not currently suse but plan to introduce	Currently use but plan to use it less	Currently use and have no plans to change usage level	Currently use and plan to use it more
Community college	52.94%	23.53%	17.65%	0.00%	0.00%	5.88%
Research university	28.57%	50.00%	14.29%	0.00%	7.14%	0.00%
MA-/PhD-granting college	33.33%	40.00%	6.67%	13.33%	0.00%	6.67%
Research university	41.18%	5.88%	0.00%	11.76%	35.29%	5.88%

142

Table 35.1.5 What are your library's plans for classroom response systems? Broken out by full-time equivalent enrollment of the college.

Enrollment	No Answer	Do not currently use nor do we plan to	Do not currently suse but plan to introduce	Currently use but plan to use it less	Currently use and have no plans to change usage level	Currently use and plan to use it more
Less than 3,000	36.84%	36.84%	15.79%	0.00%	5.26%	5.26%
10,000 or more	47.62%	38.10%	9.52%	0.00%	0.00%	4.76%
10,000 or more	34.78%	13.04%	4.35%	17.39%	26.09%	4.35%

Table 35.1.6 What are your library's plans for classroom response systems? Broken out by age of participant.

Age Range	No Answer	Do not currently use nor do we plan to	Do not currently suse but plan to introduce	Currently use but plan to use it less	Currently use and have no plans to change usage level	Currently use and plan to use it more
Under 40	47.83%	26.09%	13.04%	0.00%	4.35%	8.70%
40 to 49	27.78%	22.22%	11.11%	11.11%	22.22%	5.56%
50 and over	40.91%	36.36%	4.55%	9.09%	9.09%	0.00%

Discuss your library's experience (or your personal experience) with classroom response systems in information literacy instruction applications.

1. Have experienced technical difficulties.

2. Clickers become obsolete (in my opinion) through the use of mobile devices and PCs with applications like poll anywhere and doceri. More cost effective and just as simple to use if orchestrated properly.

3. They are Ok but being replaced by social media e.g. poll everywhere.

4. Prefer web tools for this.

5. Have used in the past, but they don't work well in shorter classes.

6. I've used these when they are part of a credit class that uses them. I have studied how to use them and still find that I need more work on them. I have posted my slides with questions on my instruction site: http://blogs.uoregon.edu/annie/

7. Good interaction and discussion generated.

8. I don't have clickers, but a show of hands or green/red cards can be just as effective and cheaper. You can also use some online apps instead.

9. More trouble than they're worth. I use PollEverywhere instead, or have students raise their hands. Our students are pretty comfortable volunteering.

10. I know there is interest, but our "discretionary" funds are being funneled into developing our learning commons. Perhaps in the future.

11. We don't see the same set of students on a regular basis - they are more one of workshops so it is very time consuming to get the students registered and set up before you can begin.

12. I am the only librarian who uses them.

13. They are useful for some classes to generate discussion and to also gauge student's level of understanding.

14. Might look at introducing a classroom response system like Socrative. I have used it but, not in the classroom yet.

15. I one time used the clickers as a voting chance for an audience award at a video contest - that was really fun and popular with the audience.

16. We don't use clickers, but use Polleverywhere. Great resource.

17. We haven't had the funds or enough stakeholder interest to try them out.

18. We've only used them for a test class. They went well, but the class was small enough that it almost seemed like extra work. The main library uses them more, but I don't know what their experience is.

19. We do not have the money to do it all, so the focus is on instruction and an open door policy in the Library. I do NOT 'enable' them, but I DO empower them.

20. We have used our Education departments set of clickers when we participated in the new student orientation sessions. The students did think using the technology was fun but since the library didn't own the equipment it was difficult to get access and the set we owned is now "old" in technological time and isn't easy to update. I would like to try some type of cell phone response but we don't always have access so I don't want to leave students out who don't have the proper technology.

21. It creates an environment where students are actively participating and are engaged with the content.

22. We tried to adopt the technology about two years ago. The person in charge of the training had not updated software, did not have working batteries in the clickers, presented very badly - he would have been our support/go-to person. It wasn't worth our time to try to get things worked out with that individual. Who is not a librarian by the way.

23. I personally have not used them. A couple of librarians tried them out and then abandoned the idea. I think it took to much time to get the students up to speed since we have limited time with students.

24. We had them for one year before I was giving instruction. They discontinued them after that year.

25. None.

26. We purchased i-clickers last year and have had a couple of trainings in using them. We plan to use them in the coming semester. Before we had clickers, we used poll everywhere and google forms in place of clickers. We have used poll everywhere and google forms for quick response to questions and also to record and display the results of group work

activities. We have found this to be a great tool to get students to respond and to facilitate discussion around concepts in our workshops.

27. We use clickers for surveying students to collect statistics on information literacy. We have also used them for games and to create teams and competitions.

28. Instead, I use free online products (like PollAnywhere) that utilize student's phones, since basically everyone has one.

29. Stduents like it - some courses require students to buy there own clickers at start of the year (refund provided at end of course).

Chapter 4 – Writing Code for Information Literacy

If your library has developed any unique or particularly effective computer codes or routines for information literacy instruction applications, please describe them.

1. I'm interested in the librarians (Kansas State and Portland State) who are using qualtrics for tutorials.

2. No, we used the old WMU SearchPath information literacy tutorials and are in the process of updating them.

3. No.

4. Nope!

5. We have several self-help learning modules for in-coming students to use to sign-up for various library services/resources.

6. http://www.staffs.ac.uk/ask

Chapter 5 – Games and Gamification

Table 36 Have you ever used games or gamification concepts (e.g. digital badges, puzzles, or role playing) in your IL instruction?

Table 36.1.1 Have you ever used games or gamification concepts (e.g. digital badges, puzzles, or role playing) in your IL instruction?

	Yes	No, but I'm interested and hope to soon	No, I'm not interested	No, I'm not familiar with this
Entire sample	44.44%	44.44%	7.94%	3.17%

Table 36.1.2 Have you ever used games or gamification concepts (e.g. digital badges, puzzles, or role playing) in your IL instruction? Broken out by public or private status of the college.

Public or Private	Yes	No, but I'm interested and hope to soon	No, I'm not interested	No, I'm not familiar with this
Public	50.00%	36.84%	7.89%	5.26%
Private	36.00%	56.00%	8.00%	0.00%

Table 36.1.3 Have you ever used games or gamification concepts (e.g. digital badges, puzzles, or role playing) in your IL instruction? Broken out by annual full-time tuition prior to any deductions.

Tuition	Yes	No, but I'm interested and hope to soon	No, I'm not interested	No, I'm not familiar with this
Less than $5,000	55.56%	33.33%	11.11%	0.00%
$5,000 to $9,999	70.00%	20.00%	0.00%	10.00%
$10,000 to $24,999	29.41%	58.82%	5.88%	5.88%
$25,000 or more	33.33%	55.56%	11.11%	0.00%

Table 36.1.4 Have you ever used games or gamification concepts (e.g. digital badges, puzzles, or role playing) in your IL instruction? Broken out by type of college.

Type of College	Yes	No, but I'm interested and hope to soon	No, I'm not interested	No, I'm not familiar with this
Community college	41.18%	47.06%	11.76%	0.00%
Research university	50.00%	42.86%	7.14%	0.00%
MA-/PhD-granting college	26.67%	60.00%	6.67%	6.67%
Research university	58.82%	29.41%	5.88%	5.88%

Table 36.1.5 Have you ever used games or gamification concepts (e.g. digital badges, puzzles, or role playing) in your IL instruction? Broken out by full-time equivalent enrollment of the college.

Enrollment	Yes	No, but I'm interested and hope to soon	No, I'm not interested	No, I'm not familiar with this
Less than 3,000	26.32%	63.16%	10.53%	0.00%
10,000 or more	52.38%	38.10%	9.52%	0.00%
10,000 or more	52.17%	34.78%	4.35%	8.70%

Table 36.1.6 Have you ever used games or gamification concepts (e.g. digital badges, puzzles, or role playing) in your IL instruction? Broken out by age of participant.

Age Range	Yes	No, but I'm interested and hope to soon	No, I'm not interested	No, I'm not familiar with this
Under 40	34.78%	65.22%	0.00%	0.00%
40 to 49	55.56%	38.89%	5.56%	0.00%
50 and over	45.45%	27.27%	18.18%	9.09%

Table 37 If you have used games or gamification concepts in your IL instruction, were they face-to-face games developed by your library or institution?*

Table 37.1.1 If you have used games or gamification concepts in your IL instruction, were they face-to-face games developed by your library or institution?

	Yes	No
Entire sample	60.71%	39.29%

Table 37.1.2 If you have used games or gamification concepts in your IL instruction, were they face-to-face games developed by your library or institution? Broken out by public or private status of the college.

Public or Private	Yes	No
Public	57.89%	42.11%
Private	66.67%	33.33%

Table 37.1.3 If you have used games or gamification concepts in your IL instruction, were they face-to-face games developed by your library or institution? Broken out by annual full-time tuition prior to any deductions.

Tuition	Yes	No
Less than $5,000	70.00%	30.00%
$5,000 to $9,999	28.57%	71.43%
$10,000 to $24,999	80.00%	20.00%
$25,000 or more	66.67%	33.33%

---

* Respondents to this question include only those participants who have used games or gamification concepts in IL instruction, as per Table 36

Table 37.1.4 If you have used games or gamification concepts in your IL instruction, were they face-to-face games developed by your library or institution? Broken out by type of college.

Type of College	Yes	No
Community college	85.71%	14.29%
4-year college	57.14%	42.86%
MA-/PhD-granting college	75.00%	25.00%
Research university	40.00%	60.00%

Table 37.1.5 If you have used games or gamification concepts in your IL instruction, were they face-to-face games developed by your library or institution? Broken out by full-time equivalent enrollment of the college.

Enrollment	Yes	No
Less than 3,000	80.00%	20.00%
3,000 to 9,999	72.73%	27.27%
10,000 or more	41.67%	58.33%

Table 37.1.6 If you have used games or gamification concepts in your IL instruction, were they face-to-face games developed by your library or institution? Broken out by age of participant.

Age Range	Yes	No
Under 40	100.00%	0.00%
40 to 49	30.00%	70.00%
50 and over	60.00%	40.00%

Table 38 If you have used games or gamification concepts in your IL instruction, were they face-to-face games developed by another library or institution?[*]

Table 38.1.1 If you have used games or gamification concepts in your IL instruction, were they face-to-face games developed by another library or institution?

	Yes	No
Entire sample	21.43%	78.57%

Table 38.1.2 If you have used games or gamification concepts in your IL instruction, were they face-to-face games developed by another library or institution? Broken out by public or private status of the college.

Public or Private	Yes	No
Public	26.32%	73.68%
Private	11.11%	88.89%

Table 38.1.3 If you have used games or gamification concepts in your IL instruction, were they face-to-face games developed by another library or institution? Broken out by annual full-time tuition prior to any deductions.

Tuition	Yes	No
Less than $5,000	40.00%	60.00%
$5,000 to $9,999	28.57%	71.43%
$10,000 to $24,999	0.00%	100.00%
$25,000 or more	0.00%	100.00%

[*] Respondents to this question include only those participants who have used games or gamification concepts in IL instruction, as per Table 36

Table 38.1.4 If you have used games or gamification concepts in your IL instruction, were they face-to-face games developed by another library or institution? Broken out by type of college.

Type of College	Yes	No
Community college	14.29%	85.71%
4-year college	42.86%	57.14%
MA-/PhD-granting college	0.00%	100.00%
Research university	20.00%	80.00%

Table 38.1.5 If you have used games or gamification concepts in your IL instruction, were they face-to-face games developed by another library or institution? Broken out by full-time equivalent enrollment of the college.

Enrollment	Yes	No
Less than 3,000	40.00%	60.00%
3,000 to 9,999	18.18%	81.82%
10,000 or more	16.67%	83.33%

Table 38.1.6 If you have used games or gamification concepts in your IL instruction, were they face-to-face games developed by another library or institution? Broken out by age of participant.

Age Range	Yes	No
Under 40	0.00%	100.00%
40 to 49	20.00%	80.00%
50 and over	40.00%	60.00%

Table 39 If you have used games or gamification concepts in your IL instruction, were they face-to-face games developed by non-library organizations?[*]

Table 39.1.1 If you have used games or gamification concepts in your IL instruction, were they face-to-face games developed by non-library organizations?

	Yes	No
Entire sample	10.71%	89.29%

Table 39.1.2 If you have used games or gamification concepts in your IL instruction, were they face-to-face games developed by non-library organizations? Broken out by public or private status of the college.

Public or Private	Yes	No
Public	15.79%	84.21%
Private	0.00%	100.00%

Table 39.1.3 If you have used games or gamification concepts in your IL instruction, were they face-to-face games developed by non-library organizations? Broken out by annual full-time tuition prior to any deductions.

Tuition	Yes	No
Less than $5,000	10.00%	90.00%
$5,000 to $9,999	14.29%	85.71%
$10,000 to $24,999	20.00%	80.00%
$25,000 or more	0.00%	100.00%

---

[*] Respondents to this question include only those participants who have used games or gamification concepts in IL instruction, as per Table 36

Table 39.1.4 If you have used games or gamification concepts in your IL instruction, were they face-to-face games developed by non-library organizations? Broken out by type of college.

Type of College	Yes	No
Community college	0.00%	100.00%
4-year college	0.00%	100.00%
MA-/PhD-granting college	0.00%	100.00%
Research university	30.00%	70.00%

Table 39.1.5 If you have used games or gamification concepts in your IL instruction, were they face-to-face games developed by non-library organizations? Broken out by full-time equivalent enrollment of the college.

Enrollment	Yes	No
Less than 3,000	0.00%	100.00%
3,000 to 9,999	0.00%	100.00%
10,000 or more	25.00%	75.00%

Table 39.1.6 If you have used games or gamification concepts in your IL instruction, were they face-to-face games developed by non-library organizations? Broken out by age of participant.

Age Range	Yes	No
Under 40	0.00%	100.00%
40 to 49	10.00%	90.00%
50 and over	20.00%	80.00%

Table 40 If you have used games or gamification concepts in your IL instruction, were they online games developed by your library or institution?[*]

Table 40.1.1 If you have used games or gamification concepts in your IL instruction, were they online games developed by your library or institution?

	Yes	No
Entire sample	17.86%	82.14%

Table 40.1.2 If you have used games or gamification concepts in your IL instruction, were they online games developed by your library or institution? Broken out by public or private status of the college.

Public or Private	Yes	No
Public	15.79%	84.21%
Private	22.22%	77.78%

Table 40.1.3 If you have used games or gamification concepts in your IL instruction, were they online games developed by your library or institution? Broken out by annual full-time tuition prior to any deductions.

Tuition	Yes	No
Less than $5,000	0.00%	100.00%
$5,000 to $9,999	14.29%	85.71%
$10,000 to $24,999	40.00%	60.00%
$25,000 or more	33.33%	66.67%

---

[*] Respondents to this question include only those participants who have used games or gamification concepts in IL instruction, as per Table 36

Table 40.1.4 If you have used games or gamification concepts in your IL instruction, were they online games developed by your library or institution? Broken out by type of college.

Type of College	Yes	No
Community college	0.00%	100.00%
4-year college	14.29%	85.71%
MA-/PhD-granting college	25.00%	75.00%
Research university	30.00%	70.00%

Table 40.1.5 If you have used games or gamification concepts in your IL instruction, were they online games developed by your library or institution? Broken out by full-time equivalent enrollment of the college.

Enrollment	Yes	No
Less than 3,000	0.00%	100.00%
3,000 to 9,999	9.09%	90.91%
10,000 or more	33.33%	66.67%

Table 40.1.6 If you have used games or gamification concepts in your IL instruction, were they online games developed by your library or institution? Broken out by age of participant.

Age Range	Yes	No
Under 40	12.50%	87.50%
40 to 49	10.00%	90.00%
50 and over	30.00%	70.00%

Table 41 If you have used games or gamification concepts in your IL instruction, were they online games developed by another library or institution?[*]

Table 41.1.1 If you have used games or gamification concepts in your IL instruction, were they online games developed by another library or institution?

	Yes	No
Entire sample	21.43%	78.57%

Table 41.1.2 If you have used games or gamification concepts in your IL instruction, were they online games developed by another library or institution? Broken out by public or private status of the college.

Public or Private	Yes	No
Public	21.05%	78.95%
Private	22.22%	77.78%

Table 41.1.3 If you have used games or gamification concepts in your IL instruction, were they online games developed by another library or institution? Broken out by annual full-time tuition prior to any deductions.

Tuition	Yes	No
Less than $5,000	10.00%	90.00%
$5,000 to $9,999	42.86%	57.14%
$10,000 to $24,999	20.00%	80.00%
$25,000 or more	16.67%	83.33%

---

[*] Respondents to this question include only those participants who have used games or gamification concepts in IL instruction, as per Table 36

Table 41.1.4 If you have used games or gamification concepts in your IL instruction, were they online games developed by another library or institution? Broken out by type of college.

Type of College	Yes	No
Community college	28.57%	71.43%
4-year college	14.29%	85.71%
MA-/PhD-granting college	0.00%	100.00%
Research university	30.00%	70.00%

Table 41.1.5 If you have used games or gamification concepts in your IL instruction, were they online games developed by another library or institution? Broken out by full-time equivalent enrollment of the college.

Enrollment	Yes	No
Less than 3,000	40.00%	60.00%
3,000 to 9,999	9.09%	90.91%
10,000 or more	25.00%	75.00%

Table 41.1.6 If you have used games or gamification concepts in your IL instruction, were they online games developed by another library or institution? Broken out by age of participant.

Age Range	Yes	No
Under 40	12.50%	87.50%
40 to 49	40.00%	60.00%
50 and over	10.00%	90.00%

Table 42 If you have used games or gamification concepts in your IL instruction, were they online games developed by non-library organizations?[*]

Table 42.1.1 If you have used games or gamification concepts in your IL instruction, were they online games developed by non-library organizations?

	Yes	No
Entire sample	0.00%	100.00%

---

[*] Respondents to this question include only those participants who have used games or gamification concepts in IL instruction, as per Table 36

Table 43 If you have used games or gamification concepts in your IL instruction, did you determine your experience to be successful thanks to a formal assessment?[*]

Table 43.1.1 If you have used games or gamification concepts in your IL instruction, did you determine your experience to be successful thanks to a formal assessment?

	Yes	No
Entire sample	17.86%	82.14%

Table 43.1.2 If you have used games or gamification concepts in your IL instruction, did you determine your experience to be successful thanks to a formal assessment? Broken out by public or private status of the college.

Public or Private	Yes	No
Public	10.53%	89.47%
Private	33.33%	66.67%

Table 43.1.3 If you have used games or gamification concepts in your IL instruction, did you determine your experience to be successful thanks to a formal assessment? Broken out by annual full-time tuition prior to any deductions.

Tuition	Yes	No
Less than $5,000	10.00%	90.00%
$5,000 to $9,999	14.29%	85.71%
$10,000 to $24,999	20.00%	80.00%
$25,000 or more	33.33%	66.67%

---

[*] Respondents to this question include only those participants who have used games or gamification concepts in IL instruction, as per Table 36

Table 43.1.4 If you have used games or gamification concepts in your IL instruction, did you determine your experience to be successful thanks to a formal assessment? Broken out by type of college.

Type of College	Yes	No
Community college	0.00%	100.00%
4-year college	14.29%	85.71%
MA-/PhD-granting college	50.00%	50.00%
Research university	20.00%	80.00%

Table 43.1.5 If you have used games or gamification concepts in your IL instruction, did you determine your experience to be successful thanks to a formal assessment? Broken out by full-time equivalent enrollment of the college.

Enrollment	Yes	No
Less than 3,000	40.00%	60.00%
3,000 to 9,999	9.09%	90.91%
10,000 or more	16.67%	83.33%

Table 43.1.6 If you have used games or gamification concepts in your IL instruction, did you determine your experience to be successful thanks to a formal assessment? Broken out by age of participant.

Age Range	Yes	No
Under 40	25.00%	75.00%
40 to 49	0.00%	100.00%
50 and over	30.00%	70.00%

Table 44 If you have used games or gamification concepts in your IL instruction, did you determine your experience to be successful thanks to an informal assessment?[*]

Table 44.1.1 If you have used games or gamification concepts in your IL instruction, did you determine your experience to be successful thanks to an informal assessment?

	Yes	No
Entire sample	32.14%	67.86%

Table 44.1.2 If you have used games or gamification concepts in your IL instruction, did you determine your experience to be successful thanks to an informal assessment? Broken out by public or private status of the college.

Public or Private	Yes	No
Public	31.58%	68.42%
Private	33.33%	66.67%

Table 44.1.3 If you have used games or gamification concepts in your IL instruction, did you determine your experience to be successful thanks to an informal assessment? Broken out by annual full-time tuition prior to any deductions.

Tuition	Yes	No
Less than $5,000	40.00%	60.00%
$5,000 to $9,999	28.57%	71.43%
$10,000 to $24,999	20.00%	80.00%
$25,000 or more	33.33%	66.67%

---

[*] Respondents to this question include only those participants who have used games or gamification concepts in IL instruction, as per Table 36

Table 44.1.4 If you have used games or gamification concepts in your IL instruction, did you determine your experience to be successful thanks to an informal assessment? Broken out by type of college.

Type of College	Yes	No
Community college	42.86%	57.14%
4-year college	42.86%	57.14%
MA-/PhD-granting college	25.00%	75.00%
Research university	20.00%	80.00%

Table 44.1.5 If you have used games or gamification concepts in your IL instruction, did you determine your experience to be successful thanks to an informal assessment? Broken out by full-time equivalent enrollment of the college.

Enrollment	Yes	No
Less than 3,000	20.00%	80.00%
3,000 to 9,999	36.36%	63.64%
10,000 or more	33.33%	66.67%

Table 44.1.6 If you have used games or gamification concepts in your IL instruction, did you determine your experience to be successful thanks to an informal assessment? Broken out by age of participant.

Age Range	Yes	No
Under 40	37.50%	62.50%
40 to 49	40.00%	60.00%
50 and over	20.00%	80.00%

Table 45 If you have used games or gamification concepts in your IL instruction, did you determine your experience to be successful thanks to positive student feedback?[*]

Table 45.1.1 If you have used games or gamification concepts in your IL instruction, did you determine your experience to be successful thanks to positive student feedback?

	Yes	No
Entire sample	60.71%	39.29%

Table 45.1.2 If you have used games or gamification concepts in your IL instruction, did you determine your experience to be successful thanks to positive student feedback? Broken out by public or private status of the college.

Public or Private	Yes	No
Public	57.89%	42.11%
Private	66.67%	33.33%

Table 45.1.3 If you have used games or gamification concepts in your IL instruction, did you determine your experience to be successful thanks to positive student feedback? Broken out by annual full-time tuition prior to any deductions.

Tuition	Yes	No
Less than $5,000	40.00%	60.00%
$5,000 to $9,999	71.43%	28.57%
$10,000 to $24,999	80.00%	20.00%
$25,000 or more	66.67%	33.33%

---

[*] Respondents to this question include only those participants who have used games or gamification concepts in IL instruction, as per Table 36

Table 45.1.4 If you have used games or gamification concepts in your IL instruction, did you determine your experience to be successful thanks to positive student feedback? Broken out by type of college.

Type of College	Yes	No
Community college	71.43%	28.57%
4-year college	42.86%	57.14%
MA-/PhD-granting college	25.00%	75.00%
Research university	80.00%	20.00%

Table 45.1.5 If you have used games or gamification concepts in your IL instruction, did you determine your experience to be successful thanks to positive student feedback? Broken out by full-time equivalent enrollment of the college.

Enrollment	Yes	No
Less than 3,000	60.00%	40.00%
3,000 to 9,999	45.45%	54.55%
10,000 or more	75.00%	25.00%

Table 45.1.6 If you have used games or gamification concepts in your IL instruction, did you determine your experience to be successful thanks to positive student feedback? Broken out by age of participant.

Age Range	Yes	No
Under 40	62.50%	37.50%
40 to 49	60.00%	40.00%
50 and over	60.00%	40.00%

Table 46 If you have used games or gamification concepts in your IL instruction, did you determine your experience to be successful thanks to it seeming like it went well?[*]

Table 46.1.1 If you have used games or gamification concepts in your IL instruction, did you determine your experience to be successful thanks to it seeming like it went well?

	Yes	No
Entire sample	35.71%	64.29%

Table 46.1.2 If you have used games or gamification concepts in your IL instruction, did you determine your experience to be successful thanks to it seeming like it went well? Broken out by public or private status of the college.

Public or Private	Yes	No
Public	42.11%	57.89%
Private	22.22%	77.78%

Table 46.1.3 If you have used games or gamification concepts in your IL instruction, did you determine your experience to be successful thanks to it seeming like it went well? Broken out by annual full-time tuition prior to any deductions.

Tuition	Yes	No
Less than $5,000	20.00%	80.00%
$5,000 to $9,999	57.14%	42.86%
$10,000 to $24,999	60.00%	40.00%
$25,000 or more	16.67%	83.33%

---

[*] Respondents to this question include only those participants who have used games or gamification concepts in IL instruction, as per Table 36

Table 46.1.4 If you have used games or gamification concepts in your IL instruction, did you determine your experience to be successful thanks to it seeming like it went well? Broken out by type of college.

Type of College	Yes	No
Community college	28.57%	71.43%
4-year college	28.57%	71.43%
MA-/PhD-granting college	25.00%	75.00%
Research university	50.00%	50.00%

Table 46.1.5 If you have used games or gamification concepts in your IL instruction, did you determine your experience to be successful thanks to it seeming like it went well? Broken out by full-time equivalent enrollment of the college.

Enrollment	Yes	No
Less than 3,000	20.00%	80.00%
3,000 to 9,999	27.27%	72.73%
10,000 or more	50.00%	50.00%

Table 46.1.6 If you have used games or gamification concepts in your IL instruction, did you determine your experience to be successful thanks to it seeming like it went well? Broken out by age of participant.

Age Range	Yes	No
Under 40	25.00%	75.00%
40 to 49	50.00%	50.00%
50 and over	30.00%	70.00%

Table 47 Did developing this game require any advanced skills or software (such as programming, graphics, Mozilla Open Badges, etc.)?[*]

Table 47.1.1 Did developing this game require any advanced skills or software (such as programming, graphics, Mozilla Open Badges, etc.)?

	No Answer	Yes	No
Entire sample	14.29%	32.14%	53.57%

Table 47.1.2 Did developing this game require any advanced skills or software (such as programming, graphics, Mozilla Open Badges, etc.)? Broken out by public or private status of the college.

Public or Private	No Answer	Yes	No
Public	21.05%	26.32%	52.63%
Private	0.00%	44.44%	55.56%

Table 47.1.3 Did developing this game require any advanced skills or software (such as programming, graphics, Mozilla Open Badges, etc.)? Broken out by annual full-time tuition prior to any deductions.

Tuition	No Answer	Yes	No
Less than $5,000	20.00%	20.00%	60.00%
$5,000 to $9,999	28.57%	14.29%	57.14%
$10,000 to $24,999	0.00%	60.00%	40.00%
$25,000 or more	0.00%	50.00%	50.00%

---

[*] Respondents to this question include only those participants who have used games or gamification concepts in IL instruction, as per Table 36

Table 47.1.4 Did developing this game require any advanced skills or software (such as programming, graphics, Mozilla Open Badges, etc.)? Broken out by type of college.

Type of College	No Answer	Yes	No
Community college	0.00%	28.57%	71.43%
Research university	28.57%	28.57%	42.86%
MA-/PhD-granting college	0.00%	25.00%	75.00%
Research university	20.00%	40.00%	40.00%

Table 47.1.5 Did developing this game require any advanced skills or software (such as programming, graphics, Mozilla Open Badges, etc.)? Broken out by full-time equivalent enrollment of the college.

Enrollment	No Answer	Yes	No
Less than 3,000	0.00%	20.00%	80.00%
10,000 or more	18.18%	27.27%	54.55%
10,000 or more	16.67%	41.67%	41.67%

Table 47.1.6 Did developing this game require any advanced skills or software (such as programming, graphics, Mozilla Open Badges, etc.)? Broken out by age of participant.

Age Range	No Answer	Yes	No
Under 40	0.00%	37.50%	62.50%
40 to 49	30.00%	20.00%	50.00%
50 and over	10.00%	40.00%	50.00%

If yes, please specify.

1. Articulate Storyline. Advanced skill level with the software.

2. Programming, video, poetry/rhyming riddles/clues.

3. It's a flash program.

4. Simple software like ppt or haiku deck (which is what I used).

5. Hotpotatoes.

6. Open Badges.

7. Quia, Captivate, etc.

Table 48 If you have used games or gamification concepts in your IL instruction, approximately how long did it take to develop this game-based project?[*]

Table 48.1.1 If you have used games or gamification concepts in your IL instruction, approximately how long did it take to develop this game-based project?

	Less than 1 day	1-7 days	More than 1 week	Don't know
Entire sample	17.86%	32.14%	17.86%	32.14%

Table 48.1.2 If you have used games or gamification concepts in your IL instruction, approximately how long did it take to develop this game-based project? Broken out by public or private status of the college.

Public or Private	Less than 1 day	1-7 days	More than 1 week	Don't know
Public	21.05%	21.05%	15.79%	42.11%
Private	11.11%	55.56%	22.22%	11.11%

Table 48.1.3 If you have used games or gamification concepts in your IL instruction, approximately how long did it take to develop this game-based project? Broken out by annual full-time tuition prior to any deductions.

Tuition	Less than 1 day	1-7 days	More than 1 week	Don't know
Less than $5,000	20.00%	30.00%	10.00%	40.00%
$5,000 to $9,999	14.29%	28.57%	14.29%	42.86%
$10,000 to $24,999	40.00%	20.00%	20.00%	20.00%
$25,000 or more	0.00%	50.00%	33.33%	16.67%

---

[*] Respondents to this question include only those participants who have used games or gamification concepts in IL instruction, as per Table 36

Table 48.1.4 If you have used games or gamification concepts in your IL instruction, approximately how long did it take to develop this game-based project? Broken out by type of college.

Type of College	Less than 1 day	1-7 days	More than 1 week	Don't know
Community college	42.86%	28.57%	14.29%	14.29%
4-year college	14.29%	42.86%	0.00%	42.86%
MA-/PhD-granting college	0.00%	75.00%	25.00%	0.00%
Research university	10.00%	10.00%	30.00%	50.00%

Table 48.1.5 If you have used games or gamification concepts in your IL instruction, approximately how long did it take to develop this game-based project? Broken out by full-time equivalent enrollment of the college.

Enrollment	Less than 1 day	1-7 days	More than 1 week	Don't know
Less than 3,000	40.00%	60.00%	0.00%	0.00%
3,000 to 9,999	18.18%	36.36%	9.09%	36.36%
10,000 or more	8.33%	16.67%	33.33%	41.67%

Table 48.1.6 If you have used games or gamification concepts in your IL instruction, approximately how long did it take to develop this game-based project? Broken out by age of participant.

Age Range	Less than 1 day	1-7 days	More than 1 week	Don't know
Under 40	25.00%	62.50%	12.50%	0.00%
40 to 49	0.00%	30.00%	10.00%	60.00%
50 and over	30.00%	10.00%	30.00%	30.00%

Briefly describe a successful game or gaming activity you have used for IL instruction.

1. Word switches.

2. We have created a quiz in which cartoon scenarios show on the screen and students use the clickers (on a timer) to submit answers and see who gets it right the fastest.

3. The Goblin Plagiarism Game from Lycoming College.

4. I use a game called "The Biggest Researcher" where the goal is to find the most relevant articles on their topic. I find that instead of giving students a topic I ask them to search on their own topic so that they leave with something that they can use in their paper. We talk about the evaluation portion - how did they determine the article was going to be valuable to their paper.

5. We have a matching game for understanding citation; we have a "Who Wants to be a Millionaire" type game to help students learn more about the Library and its policies (which had an unexpected use of being a very good training tool for student helpers).

6. Use of Jeopardy and Buzzer answer systems at the end can get the excitement going and reinforce content.

7. Students and instructors seemed to like it. Although I wonder how much students really learn and remember.

8. Build a database w/student information.

9. I use the Goblin Threat, I am not sure how effective it really is.

10. Scavenger hunt (pen and paper) for orientation groups.

11. We did an orientation scavenger hunt for Fall 2013.

12. A "search off" race between individuals who look for a website featuring specific criteria and information. Encourages application of advanced search techniques.

13. With our video game collection, we've used them for classes and for an entire credit class. These were all commercially produced video games. For a journalism class, studying the Beatles, we set up Beatles Rock Band for the students to play.

14. Info lit game.

15. In class we have students get into teams and play the online game that I created. This game has students answer questions about a given source (is this peer-reviewed, who are the authors, when was it published, is it primary or secondary, etc) to help them evaluate it. The teams get more points if they answer the questions correctly the first time. Faculty generally give the winning team extra credit points. After the game is finished we discuss the questions they had to answer in an in depth way and why those questions are useful when evaluating information.

16. Library Jeopardy.

17. We do an Amazing Library Race for orientation.

18. Boolean searching fridge magnet game.

19. I used a citation game. Several MLA citations were chosen: article, book, web source. Each citation was broken down into components and written on index cards. In class, students were broken up into groups and give sets of cards. Each group had to reassemble a citation. The group to finish first puts up their citation and the class decides if it is correct or not.

20. Media Library does the gaming activities, I am not involved in these.

21. In-class Jeopardy quiz.

22. Planning to use "The Game of Research" board game in the Fall. Developed at UT Chattanooga.

23. Clues using QR Codes.

24. Used Purdue Passport to issue digital badge for academic integrity.

25. I had a series of odd questions for students to research and see what they were able to find out in a brief amount of time. Working in groups the students drew the questions at random.

26. An ARG (alternate reality game) to teach several basic strategies, other games to indicate disciplinary areas, etc.

27. Game of teams eash representeing a resouce to buy and sell information.

What advice would you give to other librarians intrested in using games for IL instruction?

1. Electronic isn't everything; paper works great too.

2. Read about game design. Also recognize that information literacy is not exactly fun, so think about gamification as introducing motivation into an activity.

3. Make sure that student's fully grasp any directions before beginning. Specifically ask if there are questions about how the game works.

4. Don't be afraid to try.

5. Make sure that the game works on various OSs. Make sure that the game works in various browsers. Make sure that you give students instruction in how to play and what "winning" is.

6. Test before using in a classroom.

7. Can be interesting, but be careful to keep objectives clear and simple. It would be easy to get muddled in game creation and loose sight of SLOs.

8. I think that it works pretty well. Take a practical concept and make it fun for students to engage with.

9. This also can be a landmine.

10. Do what you can; keep it short; keep it light.

11. Competition does seem to drive learning for many, but leaves slower students behind. Don't make it more work for yourself than it has to be.

12. Try it!

13. Make sure that when using activities/games that they are relevant. I tried a game one semester based on Twitter and at the time we didn't have enough Twitter users (understanding of hash tags/descriptors/subject headings) to play the game effectively. I have used the game again now that there are more Twitter users or those that at least understand the hash tag system.

14. Go for it, allow enough time for development, get the classroom instructor's buy-in.

15. Develop goals, brainstorm ideas, get partners, plan ahead, evaluate.

16. Low tech F2F can work very well. Give prizes - cheep is OK.

17. Be sure and integrate it into a meaningful assignment.

18. It takes time...

Chapter 6 – Mobile Technology

How has your college used tablet computers, smartphones, and other mobile computing technologies in yor information literacy efforts?

1. We have the students use their own smart phones. We would like to get tablets.

2. We are about to create a new mobile classroom using chrome books. We have web resources that have a mobile version for mobile users.

3. Very limited. Use of phones for polling (poll everywhere, an in house system called Ripple, for clickers). We have a tablet computer for video games, used for the credit class on video games. I've also used the tablet as a whiteboard in a large lecture class and passed it around.

4. Yes, during orientation.

5. Not at this moment. We are currently using a computer lab with desktop computers for ENG 102. However, in the library I have a classroom with a single computer at a podium (which is not ideal.)

6. Introducing the catalog; showing how to use the QR codes to book a study space on library orientation tours, teaching users how to set-up & access Browzine.

7. Not really.

8. Yes, we got a set of iPads so we can turn our conference room into an additional interactive classroom, do sessions in dorms and classrooms, and support our scavenger hunts.

9. We have a mobile classroom featuring ipads and (soon) other devices for student use.

10. We don't use them at all. However, we do direct students to mobile apps from library vendors such as ebrary.

11. Every student has an ipad and we use these extensively in class.

12. We have a QR Code tour of the 1st floor of the library.

13. We have incorporated iPads into our Freshman Seminar library tour.

14. Roaming support.

15. Not yet.

16. We have used iPads and photocomic software in conjunction with the FYE programs.

Would you say that the rise of tablet computing, smartphones, and other mobile computing technologies has significantly impacted your college's purchasing plans for hardware for information literacy instruction? If so, how? Try to quantify if you can.

1. Not yet; we have tablets and e-readers for check-out, but we have not yet incorporated them into instruction.

2. Not really, other than that one batch of iPads we purchased. We did redo our site to be mobile-friendly.

3. Not at this time.

4. It is just now starting to. Faculty are getting iPads and we are investigating using them in the classroom.

5. We are planning on having laptops available for students in carts in our library classroom. I also have an information literacy class in a library classroom with one computer at a podium. It makes it very hard for the students to get the hands on practice and interaction that they need. We take turns on the computer and I guide them as they are searching for resources. The laptops will be most welcome!

6. Demand for desktop computers has not decreased as anticipated in the literature, demand for circulating iPads etc. remains high. we have used both Poll Everywhere (student devices) and clickers (library provided devices).

7. Somewhat.

8. Library staff will need more experience with these technologies so we can know how to best use them and how our students are using them.

9. No.

10. No, the College provides tablets to all students and the staff get access to educational apps as part of the education budget.

11. Yes, most definitely. We have requested funds to purchase ipads, projects, and other devices to create a uniquely mobile library instruction space.

12. No.

13. No.

14. We are in our second year of budget cuts, so we don't have much money to add them. We've had to strip them out of the budget.

15. No.

16. Yes, we purchase the newest iPads to upgrade as often as possible.

17. No, they are not interested in mobile technology.

18. Some. We have purchased a number of iPads and Windows 8 tablets and we are looking at how we can use them in IL instruction.

19. Not to my knowledge.

Chapter 7 – New Technologies

Table 49 Do you use listservs to learn about new technologies?

Table 49.1.1 Do you use listservs to learn about new technologies?

	No Answer	Yes	No
Entire sample	0.00%	76.19%	23.81%

Table 49.1.2 Do you use listservs to learn about new technologies? Broken out by public or private status of the college.

Public or Private	Yes	No
Public	78.95%	21.05%
Private	72.00%	28.00%

Table 49.1.3 Do you use listservs to learn about new technologies? Broken out by annual full-time tuition prior to any deductions.

Tuition	Yes	No
Less than $5,000	88.89%	11.11%
$5,000 to $9,999	80.00%	20.00%
$10,000 to $24,999	64.71%	35.29%
$25,000 or more	72.22%	27.78%

Table 49.1.4 Do you use listservs to learn about new technologies? Broken out by type of college.

Type of College	Yes	No
Community college	100.00%	0.00%
Research university	57.14%	42.86%
MA-/PhD-granting college	66.67%	33.33%
Research university	76.47%	23.53%

Table 49.1.5 Do you use listservs to learn about new technologies? Broken out by full-time equivalent enrollment of the college.

Enrollment	Yes	No
Less than 3,000	78.95%	21.05%
10,000 or more	71.43%	28.57%
10,000 or more	78.26%	21.74%

Table 49.1.6 Do you use listservs to learn about new technologies? Broken out by age of participant.

Age Range	Yes	No
Under 40	82.61%	17.39%
40 to 49	66.67%	33.33%
50 and over	77.27%	22.73%

Table 50 Do you use word of mouth to learn about new technologies?

Table 50.1.1 Do you use word of mouth to learn about new technologies?

	No Answer	Yes	No
Entire sample	0.00%	80.95%	19.05%

Table 50.1.2 Do you use word of mouth to learn about new technologies? Broken out by public or private status of the college.

Public or Private	Yes	No
Public	86.84%	13.16%
Private	72.00%	28.00%

Table 50.1.3 Do you use word of mouth to learn about new technologies? Broken out by annual full-time tuition prior to any deductions.

Tuition	Yes	No
Less than $5,000	94.44%	5.56%
$5,000 to $9,999	80.00%	20.00%
$10,000 to $24,999	70.59%	29.41%
$25,000 or more	77.78%	22.22%

Table 50.1.4 Do you use word of mouth to learn about new technologies? Broken out by type of college.

Type of College	Yes	No
Community college	94.12%	5.88%
Research university	64.29%	35.71%
MA-/PhD-granting college	73.33%	26.67%
Research university	88.24%	11.76%

Table 50.1.5 Do you use word of mouth to learn about new technologies? Broken out by full-time equivalent enrollment of the college.

Enrollment	Yes	No
Less than 3,000	78.95%	21.05%
10,000 or more	76.19%	23.81%
10,000 or more	86.96%	13.04%

Table 50.1.6 Do you use word of mouth to learn about new technologies? Broken out by age of participant.

Age Range	Yes	No
Under 40	86.96%	13.04%
40 to 49	83.33%	16.67%
50 and over	72.73%	27.27%

Table 51 Do you use publications to learn about new technologies?

Table 51.1.1 Do you use publications to learn about new technologies?

	No Answer	Yes	No
Entire sample	0.00%	68.25%	31.75%

Table 51.1.2 Do you use publications to learn about new technologies? Broken out by public or private status of the college.

Public or Private	Yes	No
Public	78.95%	21.05%
Private	52.00%	48.00%

Table 51.1.3 Do you use publications to learn about new technologies? Broken out by annual full-time tuition prior to any deductions.

Tuition	Yes	No
Less than $5,000	88.89%	11.11%
$5,000 to $9,999	70.00%	30.00%
$10,000 to $24,999	58.82%	41.18%
$25,000 or more	55.56%	44.44%

Table 51.1.4 Do you use publications to learn about new technologies? Broken out by type of college.

Type of College	Yes	No
Community college	94.12%	5.88%
Research university	57.14%	42.86%
MA-/PhD-granting college	46.67%	53.33%
Research university	70.59%	29.41%

Table 51.1.5 Do you use publications to learn about new technologies? Broken out by full-time equivalent enrollment of the college.

Enrollment	Yes	No
Less than 3,000	57.89%	42.11%
10,000 or more	71.43%	28.57%
10,000 or more	73.91%	26.09%

Table 51.1.6 Do you use publications to learn about new technologies? Broken out by age of participant.

Age Range	Yes	No
Under 40	78.26%	21.74%
40 to 49	55.56%	44.44%
50 and over	68.18%	31.82%

Table 52 Do you use online social networks (Twitter, Facebook, etc.) to learn about new technologies?

Table 52.1.1 Do you use online social networks (Twitter, Facebook, etc.) to learn about new technologies?

	No Answer	Yes	No
Entire sample	0.00%	50.79%	49.21%

Table 52.1.2 Do you use online social networks (Twitter, Facebook, etc.) to learn about new technologies? Broken out by public or private status of the college.

Public or Private	Yes	No
Public	52.63%	47.37%
Private	48.00%	52.00%

Table 52.1.3 Do you use online social networks (Twitter, Facebook, etc.) to learn about new technologies? Broken out by annual full-time tuition prior to any deductions.

Tuition	Yes	No
Less than $5,000	50.00%	50.00%
$5,000 to $9,999	20.00%	80.00%
$10,000 to $24,999	64.71%	35.29%
$25,000 or more	55.56%	44.44%

Table 52.1.4 Do you use online social networks (Twitter, Facebook, etc.) to learn about new technologies? Broken out by type of college.

Type of College	Yes	No
Community college	41.18%	58.82%
Research university	57.14%	42.86%
MA-/PhD-granting college	53.33%	46.67%
Research university	52.94%	47.06%

Table 52.1.5 Do you use online social networks (Twitter, Facebook, etc.) to learn about new technologies? Broken out by full-time equivalent enrollment of the college.

Enrollment	Yes	No
Less than 3,000	47.37%	52.63%
10,000 or more	38.10%	61.90%
10,000 or more	65.22%	34.78%

Table 52.1.6 Do you use online social networks (Twitter, Facebook, etc.) to learn about new technologies? Broken out by age of participant.

Age Range	Yes	No
Under 40	73.91%	26.09%
40 to 49	55.56%	44.44%
50 and over	22.73%	77.27%

Table 53 Do you use conferences to learn about new technologies?

Table 53.1.1 Do you use conferences to learn about new technologies?

	No Answer	Yes	No
Entire sample	0.00%	85.71%	14.29%

Table 53.1.2 Do you use conferences to learn about new technologies? Broken out by public or private status of the college.

Public or Private	Yes	No
Public	89.47%	10.53%
Private	80.00%	20.00%

Table 53.1.3 Do you use conferences to learn about new technologies? Broken out by annual full-time tuition prior to any deductions.

Tuition	Yes	No
Less than $5,000	94.44%	5.56%
$5,000 to $9,999	70.00%	30.00%
$10,000 to $24,999	82.35%	17.65%
$25,000 or more	88.89%	11.11%

Table 53.1.4 Do you use conferences to learn about new technologies? Broken out by type of college.

Type of College	Yes	No
Community college	88.24%	11.76%
Research university	85.71%	14.29%
MA-/PhD-granting college	80.00%	20.00%
Research university	88.24%	11.76%

Table 53.1.5 Do you use conferences to learn about new technologies? Broken out by full-time equivalent enrollment of the college.

Enrollment	Yes	No
Less than 3,000	73.68%	26.32%
10,000 or more	90.48%	9.52%
10,000 or more	91.30%	8.70%

Table 53.1.6 Do you use conferences to learn about new technologies? Broken out by age of participant.

Age Range	Yes	No
Under 40	91.30%	8.70%
40 to 49	88.89%	11.11%
50 and over	77.27%	22.73%

If you use another platform not listed above to learn about new technologies, please specify.

1. Students and young/tech savvy librarians.

2. Student employees.

3. Following InfoToday and InfoDocket ResearchBuzz.

4. Research.

5. IDT online masters program.

Table 54 Are time limitations a barrier or obstacle you face when trying to use new technologies in IL instruction?

Table 54.1.1 Are time limitations a barrier or obstacle you face when trying to use new technologies in IL instruction?

	No Answer	Yes	No
Entire sample	0.00%	77.78%	22.22%

Table 54.1.2 Are time limitations a barrier or obstacle you face when trying to use new technologies in IL instruction? Broken out by public or private status of the college.

Public or Private	Yes	No
Public	81.58%	18.42%
Private	72.00%	28.00%

Table 54.1.3 Are time limitations a barrier or obstacle you face when trying to use new technologies in IL instruction? Broken out by annual full-time tuition prior to any deductions.

Tuition	Yes	No
Less than $5,000	72.22%	27.78%
$5,000 to $9,999	80.00%	20.00%
$10,000 to $24,999	88.24%	11.76%
$25,000 or more	72.22%	27.78%

Table 54.1.4 Are time limitations a barrier or obstacle you face when trying to use new technologies in IL instruction? Broken out by type of college.

Type of College	Yes	No
Community college	82.35%	17.65%
Research university	78.57%	21.43%
MA-/PhD-granting college	73.33%	26.67%
Research university	76.47%	23.53%

Table 54.1.5 Are time limitations a barrier or obstacle you face when trying to use new technologies in IL instruction? Broken out by full-time equivalent enrollment of the college.

Enrollment	Yes	No
Less than 3,000	78.95%	21.05%
10,000 or more	80.95%	19.05%
10,000 or more	73.91%	26.09%

Table 54.1.6 Are time limitations a barrier or obstacle you face when trying to use new technologies in IL instruction? Broken out by age of participant.

Age Range	Yes	No
Under 40	78.26%	21.74%
40 to 49	77.78%	22.22%
50 and over	77.27%	22.73%

Table 55 Are institutional buy-ins a barrier or obstacle you face when trying to use new technologies in IL instruction?

Table 55.1.1 Are institutional buy-ins a barrier or obstacle you face when trying to use new technologies in IL instruction?

	No Answer	Yes	No
Entire sample	0.00%	47.62%	52.38%

Table 55.1.2 Are institutional buy-ins a barrier or obstacle you face when trying to use new technologies in IL instruction? Broken out by public or private status of the college.

Public or Private	Yes	No
Public	47.37%	52.63%
Private	48.00%	52.00%

Table 55.1.3 Are institutional buy-ins a barrier or obstacle you face when trying to use new technologies in IL instruction? Broken out by annual full-time tuition prior to any deductions.

Tuition	Yes	No
Less than $5,000	50.00%	50.00%
$5,000 to $9,999	60.00%	40.00%
$10,000 to $24,999	29.41%	70.59%
$25,000 or more	55.56%	44.44%

Table 55.1.4 Are institutional buy-ins a barrier or obstacle you face when trying to use new technologies in IL instruction? Broken out by type of college.

Type of College	Yes	No
Community college	47.06%	52.94%
Research university	28.57%	71.43%
MA-/PhD-granting college	46.67%	53.33%
Research university	64.71%	35.29%

Table 55.1.5 Are institutional buy-ins a barrier or obstacle you face when trying to use new technologies in IL instruction? Broken out by full-time equivalent enrollment of the college.

Enrollment	Yes	No
Less than 3,000	36.84%	63.16%
10,000 or more	42.86%	57.14%
10,000 or more	60.87%	39.13%

Table 55.1.6 Are institutional buy-ins a barrier or obstacle you face when trying to use new technologies in IL instruction? Broken out by age of participant.

Age Range	Yes	No
Under 40	65.22%	34.78%
40 to 49	44.44%	55.56%
50 and over	31.82%	68.18%

Table 56 Are costs of equipment or software a barrier or obstacle you face when trying to use new technologies in IL instruction?

Table 56.1.1 Are costs of equipment or software a barrier or obstacle you face when trying to use new technologies in IL instruction?

	No Answer	Yes	No
Entire sample	0.00%	73.02%	26.98%

Table 56.1.2 Are costs of equipment or software a barrier or obstacle you face when trying to use new technologies in IL instruction? Broken out by public or private status of the college.

Public or Private	Yes	No
Public	76.32%	23.68%
Private	68.00%	32.00%

Table 56.1.3 Are costs of equipment or software a barrier or obstacle you face when trying to use new technologies in IL instruction? Broken out by annual full-time tuition prior to any deductions.

Tuition	Yes	No
Less than $5,000	77.78%	22.22%
$5,000 to $9,999	70.00%	30.00%
$10,000 to $24,999	76.47%	23.53%
$25,000 or more	66.67%	33.33%

Table 56.1.4 Are costs of equipment or software a barrier or obstacle you face when trying to use new technologies in IL instruction? Broken out by type of college.

Type of College	Yes	No
Community college	94.12%	5.88%
Research university	42.86%	57.14%
MA-/PhD-granting college	73.33%	26.67%
Research university	76.47%	23.53%

Table 56.1.5 Are costs of equipment or software a barrier or obstacle you face when trying to use new technologies in IL instruction? Broken out by full-time equivalent enrollment of the college.

Enrollment	Yes	No
Less than 3,000	68.42%	31.58%
10,000 or more	71.43%	28.57%
10,000 or more	78.26%	21.74%

Table 56.1.6 Are costs of equipment or software a barrier or obstacle you face when trying to use new technologies in IL instruction? Broken out by age of participant.

Age Range	Yes	No
Under 40	65.22%	34.78%
40 to 49	77.78%	22.22%
50 and over	77.27%	22.73%

Table 57 Are technical abilities a barrier or obstacle you face when trying to use new technologies in IL instruction?

Table 57.1.1 Are technical abilities a barrier or obstacle you face when trying to use new technologies in IL instruction?

	No Answer	Yes	No
Entire sample	0.00%	46.03%	53.97%

Table 57.1.2 Are technical abilities a barrier or obstacle you face when trying to use new technologies in IL instruction? Broken out by public or private status of the college.

Public or Private	Yes	No
Public	52.63%	47.37%
Private	36.00%	64.00%

Table 57.1.3 Are technical abilities a barrier or obstacle you face when trying to use new technologies in IL instruction? Broken out by annual full-time tuition prior to any deductions.

Tuition	Yes	No
Less than $5,000	61.11%	38.89%
$5,000 to $9,999	50.00%	50.00%
$10,000 to $24,999	35.29%	64.71%
$25,000 or more	38.89%	61.11%

Table 57.1.4 Are technical abilities a barrier or obstacle you face when trying to use new technologies in IL instruction? Broken out by type of college.

Type of College	Yes	No
Community college	52.94%	47.06%
Research university	42.86%	57.14%
MA-/PhD-granting college	53.33%	46.67%
Research university	35.29%	64.71%

Table 57.1.5 Are technical abilities a barrier or obstacle you face when trying to use new technologies in IL instruction? Broken out by full-time equivalent enrollment of the college.

Enrollment	Yes	No
Less than 3,000	31.58%	68.42%
10,000 or more	61.90%	38.10%
10,000 or more	43.48%	56.52%

Table 57.1.6 Are technical abilities a barrier or obstacle you face when trying to use new technologies in IL instruction? Broken out by age of participant.

Age Range	Yes	No
Under 40	39.13%	60.87%
40 to 49	38.89%	61.11%
50 and over	59.09%	40.91%

If there are any other barriers or obstacles you face in trying to use new technologies in IL instruction, please specify.

1. Since none of us have much programming background, we have to rely on previously existing software.

2. Librarian buy-in (not sure if that is included in "institutional buy-in" but I think the institution is sometimes more ready to use new technologies than the library teachers.

3. Not so much technical ability as technical barriers (i.e., campus IT).

4. Need faculty buy-in for assigning 'flipped' materials before class, which can be difficult to get.

5. Uncertain how course instructor will react to something different.

6. How to make sure we have a plan for using them effectively before making the purchase, that it won't just be trendy with no positive learning outcomes.

Please tell us about any other new technologies or instructional strategies that you have been using successfully in your IL instruction that were not addressed in this survey.

1. Not sure if this counts -- I have created an activity where students are asked to work in groups to evaluate resources for scholarly vs. non scholarly and then use polleverywhere to share their analysis with the class in real time. This was a class already given iPads on a special institutional grant.

2. We're starting to use Guide on the Side tutorials.

3. The goal of the advanced comp class is to write a research paper on a topic of the student's choosing. We have found this to be successful as the students are interested in the topic they are writing about. We also have our students present the finding of their research paper through a brief presentation incorporating a multimedia resource video or music that relates to their topic. This has worked very well and we have gotten a nice response from the students.

4. Polleverywhere is probably the best we've used.

5. The University is using Elluminate for webinar type sessions and Panopto for screen recordings. The Library staff is also using Snag-it and Jing.

6. We have developed tutorials using Camtasia and Screencast-O-Matic.

7. This survey is well ahead of me and my staff in terms of technology.

8. This isn't a direct application of technology in the classroom, but I have started using concepts related to social media to explain IL concepts. For example, the @ attribution in social media is similar to an in-text citation.

9. Tutorial creation software such as Captivate.

10. Tutorials, flipped classrooms, Click Share (allows student computers to display on screen in front of class), classroom design in the round (with 5 screens on surrounding walls), touch screen podium technology.

11. I teach mostly media literacy workshops and specifically do workshops based on projects classes are doing. I have been finding that giving students the chance to critique each other's work is very helpful - I find they often will share insights or technology skills with each other during those times.

12. We just purchased Information Literacy Course Modules from Credo, and these will be used heavily to support IL instruction.

13. Looking at producing an iBook for use at induction instead of Powerpoint.

14. LibGuides, Blackboard Learn, instructional videos.

15. Social media as a space in which to help students develop metacognitive awareness of their own information processes and behaviors.

Table 58 Are there any technologies that you have tried using for IL instruction that were not successful?

Table 58.1.1 Are there any technologies that you have tried using for IL instruction that were not successful?

	No Answer	Yes	No
Entire sample	33.33%	14.29%	52.38%

Table 58.1.2 Are there any technologies that you have tried using for IL instruction that were not successful? Broken out by public or private status of the college.

Public or Private	No Answer	Yes	No
Public	21.05%	21.05%	57.89%
Private	52.00%	4.00%	44.00%

Table 58.1.3 Are there any technologies that you have tried using for IL instruction that were not successful? Broken out by annual full-time tuition prior to any deductions.

Tuition	No Answer	Yes	No
Less than $5,000	11.11%	16.67%	72.22%
$5,000 to $9,999	60.00%	0.00%	40.00%
$10,000 to $24,999	29.41%	29.41%	41.18%
$25,000 or more	44.44%	5.56%	50.00%

Table 58.1.4 Are there any technologies that you have tried using for IL instruction that were not successful? Broken out by type of college.

Type of College	No Answer	Yes	No
Community college	11.76%	11.76%	76.47%
Research university	50.00%	14.29%	35.71%
MA-/PhD-granting college	46.67%	6.67%	46.67%
Research university	29.41%	23.53%	47.06%

Table 58.1.5 Are there any technologies that you have tried using for IL instruction that were not successful? Broken out by full-time equivalent enrollment of the college.

Enrollment	No Answer	Yes	No
Less than 3,000	31.58%	5.26%	63.16%
10,000 or more	47.62%	19.05%	33.33%
10,000 or more	21.74%	17.39%	60.87%

Table 58.1.6 Are there any technologies that you have tried using for IL instruction that were not successful? Broken out by age of participant.

Age Range	No Answer	Yes	No
Under 40	26.09%	4.35%	69.57%
40 to 49	33.33%	22.22%	44.44%
50 and over	40.91%	18.18%	40.91%

If yes, please explain.

1. They're all unsuccessful to *some* extent...the point is to iterate on them and figure out how they work best for you and your institution. Sometimes flipping the classroom results in the students not doing the homework beforehand if you don't have 100% faculty buy-in, and then those students have to catch up to the rest. Some of our databases don't work on the iPads.

2. My videos aren't always successful. I'm getting better, but it's still a learning process.

3. I tried for 3 terms to have students bring readings/text to class using their devices and found that it didn't really work. This term, I brought in (literally) reams of paper and thought the class was much more engaged and on task. (sigh)

4. Quite a while back I was concerned with people ignoring instruction and going on facebook and such during classes. I tried doing things like controlling screens or locking screens with remote desktop application and then unlocking when the time came for practice but it was cumbersome and difficult to manage while teaching - I've since dropped it and rely on GAs or instructors to monitor students and go at it with the understanding that if the student really wants to ignore the instruction and play on the laptop they are going to.

5. Using visualizers never really worked out for us. We stopped using overhead projectors & transparencies years ago.

6. The clicker experience.

7. Clickers. Cumbersome, clumsy, unreliable system.

8. We've given up on smart boards and mobile tablets.

9. I have had some issues with web based tools in the classroom such as Wordle and Knight Cite.

10. Tried PollEverywhere, but had technical difficulties executing once in the class.

Made in the USA
Lexington, KY
29 September 2015